HEALING A BROKEN NATION

TEACHING AND PREACHING FORGIVENESS AND RECONCILIATION

JAMES PHILLIP SMITH

WESTBOW
PRESS®
A DIVISION OF THOMAS NELSON
& ZONDERVAN

WestBow Press books may be ordered through booksellers or by contacting:

WestBow Press
A Division of Thomas Nelson & Zondervan
1663 Liberty Drive
Bloomington, IN 47403
www.westbowpress.com
844-714-3454

ISBN: 978-1-6642-3847-3 (sc)
ISBN: 978-1-6642-3846-6 (hc)
ISBN: 978-1-6642-3848-0 (e)

Library of Congress Control Number: 2021913075

Print information available on the last page.

WestBow Press rev. date: 07/28/2021

In loving memory of my mother, Laura, who inspired in me the love of Christ Jesus.

CONTENTS

ACKNOWLEDGMENTS

This book is the result of lessons I learned over three challenging years of study at the Chicago Theological Seminary, twenty-five years of ministry in churches, and my life experiences as well as those of parishioners and others willing to share them with me.

The following are only a few of the many people whose support, suggestions, critiques, ideas, and other contributions were vital to this book. I wish to express my sincere gratitude to:

My loving and caring wife, Millie N. Smith.

Pamela, Marlina, and Tyrel, my lovely children, who wished Daddy well as I traveled for three years on Fathers' Day to residency.

The gifted professors who transformed my preaching style and challenged me to go beyond outside the box, especially Kirk Byron Jones, Dow Edgerton, Charlie Cosgrove, and Frank Thomas.

To you, who have chosen to read this book, be encouraged.

> I BESEECH you therefore, brethren {sisters}, by the mercies of God, that you present your bodies a living sacrifice, holy, acceptable unto God, which is your reasonable service. And be not conformed to this world: but be you transformed by the renewing of your mind, that you may prove what is that good, and acceptable, and perfect, will of God. (Romans 12:1–2 NIV)

PREFACE

Utilizing a paradigm of appropriation is the model that has evolved as this work has been done. This model creates a parallel between the biblical context, the preacher's or teacher's context, and the context of the community. Using this model is how the gospel becomes relevant for listeners.

With the main theme being The Past: Face It, Embrace It, and Kiss It Goodbye, this work uses this theme to create a parallel for preaching and teaching forgiveness and reconciliation to bring about transformation. These three elements are what ultimately lead to healing and wholeness.

The Past: Face It is preaching forgiveness; The Past: Embrace It is preaching reconciliation; and The Past: Kiss It Goodbye is preaching transformation. This thread has been woven throughout reaching into the cognitive, emotive, and intuitive areas of the people involved.

This work, as God's Word is intended to, has not returned void. Areas of heartache and pain have been sought out, reached into, and drawn out. As a result, those involved in this process will never be the same. Through the gospel, people have been allowed the opportunity to acknowledge their hurt or loss, grieve, and ultimately move on.

To achieve forgiveness, the past must be recognized. Those things that have hurt, wounded, and caused deep scars are buried in the past. Dredging them up requires engagement that reaches into the depths of the cognitive and the emotive areas of the people involved and pulling those things to the surface so the grief process can take place. Whether it be grief over a broken relationship or some other disappointment or loss, recognizing that the pain is there is key in the process of letting go.

When preaching forgiveness, the lesson that is to be learned is that once we have faced the pain of the past, it has to be accepted for what it is, processed, and then released. Holding onto that pain and bitterness only hinders us from being able to live in the now and to prepare to step into our future. This work has led to a model that has been tried and tested and proves to be transformative when the work is done with honesty and sincerity.

If people are going to live their lives in fullness and wholeness, allowing themselves to let go of past hurts and disappointments is imperative. Embodied in this work are four models that address forgiveness and reconciliation: the theory of change, the grief model, and the teaching model wrapped up in and driven by the homiletical model, which is outlined in the beginning of this preface. The other three are as follows.

Theory of Change

This model involves identifying the long-term goal, which in this case is transformation. This is the overarching theme and desired end of the entire process. To arrive there, the historical context has to be revisited to identify what has transpired and what needs to be addressed to achieve the desired goal. From there, identifying how to proceed is the next step. To do this, a parish project group was formed and involved during the process to ensure that the assumptions made and the processes used would be based on inclusion of the community involved and not on assumptions that were made based on hypothetical information. Realizing that this community of faith was struggling to live an abundant life was the outside observation. It would take the inside confirmation to help determine the process that would lead to healing and wholeness.

Grief Model

To release pain, hurt, and resentment, grieving has to take place. When occurrences such as those presented in these cases have taken place, often, the opportunity to dialogue, vent, or otherwise discuss any perceived injustices or wrongs has not been afforded. In this process, people have had an opportunity to reopen and discuss current issues or some that have been buried deep in their past.

The Past: Face It presented an opportunity for parishioners to reflect on those issues with which they had not dealt and come to terms with them realizing that sometimes, the only party involved may be them alone.

Teaching Model

Utilizing the model of sermons and current events that have evolved from open-forum discussion and Bible study became the process for preaching and teaching. Taking the biblical story, my own story, and incorporating the stories of people in the congregation helped to make the scriptures relevant. This allowed the opportunity to use the homiletical model to bring about a paradigm shift concerning forgiveness and reconciliation.

The claim of this book is that where there is perceived betrayal that inflicts pain, hurt, disappointment, lack of trust, and stagnation in a relationship, organization, congregation, or other group, preaching and teaching on forgiveness, reconciliation, and transformation can lead to healing and wholeness. It is crucial to include all age levels in small-group studies. What blocks us from the way of forgiveness does not lie in the unreadiness of the one who has been wronged to forgive but in the inability of the one who has done wrong to receive forgiveness. Keeping this in mind, through preaching and small-group studies, the learners and hearers will recount old fears, recognize their unworthiness, experience the scripture, and believe and receive forgiveness as a result of God's love.

God created humanity to be in relationship to gain revelation. Furthermore, the preacher and parish project group working closely together is an effective tool in the process to form and shape the sermons and lessons in a way that makes it possible for more people to be touched.

> Two are better than one ... if one falls, the other can help. (Ecclesiastes 4:9–10 NKJV)

INTRODUCTION

In churches and families, we find people of varied backgrounds and socioeconomic status. They are educators, politicians, business owners, nurses, doctors, lawyers, food service workers, administrators, and industrial workers. These are people of great resources, gifts, and talents who have the potential to transform their communities from the inside out. Over time, however, it has become increasingly difficult for them to work together to be lights in their communities.

A further look into the situation reveals great potential. It gives the impression of a pot of water just at the boiling point but seemingly unable to boil. As time is spent with this congregation, family, or individuals, it becomes evident that there are deep-rooted issues of unresolved conflict and disappointment that have brought them to that point.

Due to the history of hurts and disappointments, a root of bitterness can develop in a person, community, or a congregation that can cause them to stagnate. Conflict that has taken place between laity and clergy, among parishioners, and among families has led to a lack of trust and feelings of betrayal. These issues present themselves as the congregation or family tries to move forward together.

When churches experience betrayals of trust involving allegations of infidelity, sexual abuse, pastors who refuse to perform their pastoral duties until they receive their paychecks, leaders who refuse to serve because they are angry with the pastor or someone in the congregation, and because of past accusations of improper handling of funds by laity and/or clergy, that creates a toxic environment of mistrust. This environment has not been healthy. It has created a mentality among some parishioners that they must keep the pastor under control.

Factions of families against families have also existed. Therefore, the past hurts, angers, and disappointments have been handed down through families and projected onto each pastor that has come into the parish. Pastors are viewed as spiritual as well as community leaders. Some parishioners find that the way the laity and the leadership in the church handle conflict regarding the pastor is harsh and disrespectful. To this end, unforgiveness and broken relationships keep believers from being able to fully respond to their call to ministry in their community and in the world.

The Word of God has transforming power. The scriptures tell us,

> As the rain and snow come down from heaven, and do not return to it without watering the earth and making it bud and flourish, so that it yields seed for the sower and bread for the eater, so is my word that goes out from my mouth: it shall not return void, but will accomplish what I desire and achieve the purpose for which I sent it. (Isaiah 55:10–11 NIV)

It brought about transformation in my life concerning my broken relationship with my father and my call to preach, and I believe that God forgave me, so I needed to forgive my father.

Teaching and preaching transform people's hearts and allow them to live in the freedom that God intended. Preaching can set the people of God free. With this in mind, the focus of this book becomes preaching and teaching forgiveness and reconciliation that leads to healing and wholeness, which is much needed in our nation and the world.

In a time of such moral decay, lack of compassion, mass shootings, racial conflict, sexual misconduct, assault and harassment, and global uncertainty due to political ideologies, the world is hurting. Healing needs to take place on many levels, but it must begin with forgiveness. The starting point of forgiveness is genuine dialogue and vulnerability. On the cross, Jesus said, "Father, forgive them, for they do not know what they are doing" (Luke 23:34 NKJV).

There exists a lack of understanding about forgiveness that can block us from being able to forgive. It is not about the unreadiness or unwillingness of the person who was wronged to forgive but the inability of the one who has done wrong to acknowledge that. Keeping this in mind, hearers will recount old fears, recognize their unworthiness, believe, and receive forgiveness experienced as a result of God's love. Therefore, focusing sermons, small-group learning, and Bible study on forgiveness can bring about healing and wholeness resulting in healthier individuals, families, congregations, and communities.

CHAPTER 1

FORGIVENESS

For if you forgive men when they sin against you, your
heavenly Father will also forgive you. But if you do not
forgive men their sins, your Father will not forgive your
sin. (Matthew 6:14–15 NIV)

Forgiveness is critical in restoring broken relationships and an important
ingredient for healing and wholeness to take place. Forgiveness begins
when the one who had inflicted the pain and the one who had been
hurt recognize and acknowledge the depth of the injury and assess the
damage.

The *Concise American Heritage Dictionary* defines forgiveness as
excusing a fault or offense; pardon; no longer feeling anger or resentment;

to absolve from payment of.[1] *Webster's* concurs but adds, "allowing room for error or weakness."[2]

Forgiveness can be defined by what it is not. Forgiveness is not allowing oneself to be taken advantage of or abused; it is not a license to continue to injure or to do wrong knowing that you will be forgiven. While forgiveness may seem to be an act of selfless, unconditional love, it has benefits for all parties involved.

Jesus gave us the biblical model for forgiveness in Matthew 6:12 (NIV): "Forgive us our debts, as we also have forgiven our debtors." This topic was important enough to warrant further commentary by Jesus after the conclusion of the prayer: "For if you forgive men when they sin against you, your heavenly Father will also forgive you. But if you do not forgive men their sins, your Father will not forgive your sin" (Matthew 6:14–15 NIV).

Some view forgiveness as a way of making things right with God, and to a certain extent, that holds truth. However, a more accurate view of forgiveness is wrapped up in community. God calls us to live in community. Through sin, we are broken. L. Gregory Jones, author of *Embodying Forgiveness: A Theological Analysis*, wrote,

> The purpose of forgiveness is the restoration of communion, the reconciliation of brokenness. Neither should forgiveness be confined to a word to be spoken, a feeling to be felt, or an isolated action to be done; rather, it involves a way of life to be lived in fidelity to God's Kingdom.[3]

---

[1] *The Concise American Heritage Dictionary*, revised edition. Houghton Mifflin, 1987, 276.

[2] *Merriam-Webster's Collegiate Dictionary*, tenth edition, 2001, 457.

[3] Jones, L. Gregory. *Embodying Forgiveness: A Theological Analysis*. Grand Rapids, MI: William B. Eerdmans, 1995. 5.

People need to experience healing. For that to happen, they must first be able to give and receive forgiveness. When we recognize the need for forgiveness, we restore broken fellowship and receive forgiveness that we experience as a result of God's love. Therefore, preaching and teaching forgiveness lead to transformation that brings about healing and wholeness.

Preaching and Teaching Forgiveness for Transformation

Preaching and teaching can transform the hearts of people and allow them to live their lives in the freedom that God intended. Then what must preaching and teaching involve? Who must be at the table to experience the scripture that can effect change? How do we experience the scripture? In *Speak to Me That I May Speak*, Dow Edgerton wrote about interpretation and spiritual praxis and used the analogy of becoming what you eat to illustrate transformation.

> We eat bread and become bread. The transformation is mutual, the bread into the eater, the eater into the bread. So with this work of interpretation: the praxis of your interpretation becomes the story of your life, and the story of your life becomes the praxis of your interpretation.[4]

Providing this bread to the congregation in such a way that they feed on it and experience transformation in the area of understanding forgiveness becomes the task of the preacher or teacher. The teacher's or

---

[4] W. Dow Edgerton. *O Speak to Me That I May Speak: A Spirituality of Preaching.* Cleveland: Pilgrim Press, 2006, 17.

preacher's story along with the stories of the congregation and others—i.e., youth, adults, seniors, and people from the wider community—become the larger story that shapes and frames the understanding of forgiveness for the larger body of believers. For this process to work and have a lasting effect, a group of people who represent a thorough cross section of the community should be formed. This group should comprise all age levels, regular and irregular attendees, leaders, and others so that they will have their input taken into consideration. It is this team that will be key to affect healing, wholeness, and transformation.

How listeners hear the Word of God in stories and relate it to their lives sets the stage for embodying and experiencing the grace of God that brings about transformation. The challenge becomes bringing the various perspectives together in a cohesive way that makes sense to the congregation. Having to use the interpretations provided by the group members is a very humbling experience as well as a powerful lesson. It takes you into an area of trust where you have to review what they have provided and with an open mind discern whether the interpretation remained true to the text. The preachers or teachers will have to open themselves up to looking at the text from other perspectives yet still be able to challenge or take issue with statements or perspectives that do not hold to the text or have not been carefully researched.

Be careful not to include anything that would be contradictory or bring confusion to the congregation. Your task is to make sure that it makes sense, connects well, and remains true to the text. Yes, a powerful lesson learned—when you fire a shotgun, the buckshot starts out small, but the farther it travels, the more of the target it hits. "Two are better than one" (Ecclesiastes 4:9a NKJV).

To provide some practical assistance to move forward in this process, we dissected several passages of scripture on forgiveness. The first three led to a sermon series on the past. They are The Past: Face It (Genesis 32:13–21), The Past: Embrace It (Luke 15:11–20), and The Past: Kiss It Goodbye (Genesis 45:14–15). Following are breakdowns of the sermons with teaching points. The full sermon manuscripts can be found in the appendices.

SERMON 1

The Past: Face It

FEET ON BROKEN GLASS

The road to forgiveness starts by our recognizing that we have pain and issues from our past that seem to affect us every day. These issues can hold us back from enjoying the present and from fully realizing the future into which God is calling us. If parishioners, communities, and families are willing to face their past hurts, work with the facilitator, and be open to the working of the Holy Spirit, they can begin the process of forgiveness.

In the first sermon, an opportunity to experience forgiveness was given to parishioners. This sermon contains the story of Jacob and Esau. Through the traditional reading of the scripture, dynamic translation, and life examples, the story of Jacob's fear of meeting his brother after twenty years was told.

Because the traditional reading of the key verse was done, those who were older and more knowledgeable of the scriptures could grasp the story. That along with examples that are relevant to the lives of people in the community of faith made the text relevant and real. We used examples such as being overlooked for a position in the workplace, disputes with family members over handling the finances of a loved one who has passed on, and people who had bad experiences in school and even as adults and avoiding those who had hurt them. These examples drew the congregation into the text and helped them experience it in light of their experiences.

In addition to the traditional reading, which drew in the adults, the process of dynamic translation was introduced. Dynamic translation communicates the basic message of the biblical text using modern language and expression. The dynamic translation presented by the youth provided an opportunity for younger parishioners to hear the scripture in their language and find it relevant to their culture. Their expression of the scripture in a contemporary way included the slang of today and the clothes and popular fashions of today. Following is the traditional reading as well as the dynamic translation done by the youth of the Genesis 32:13–21 passage.

> For he thought, I may appease him with the present that goes ahead of me, and afterwards I shall see his face, perhaps he will accept me. (Genesis 32:20b NRSV)

Traditional Reading	Dynamic Translation
He spent the night there, and from what he had with him he selected a gift for his brother Esau: two hundred female goats and twenty male goats, two hundred ewes and twenty rams, Thirty female camels with their young, forty cows and ten bulls, and twenty female donkeys and ten male donkeys. He put them in the care of his servants, each herd by itself, and said to his servants, "Go ahead of me, and keep some space between the herds."	In the darkness of the midnight hour and from his store at the mall, Jacob selected gifts for his brother. One beautiful gold cross and three silver keys, two pairs of Timberlands, four pairs of Jordans, twenty SpongeBob SquarePants shirts, two pairs of Air Force Ones, two Tommy shirts, and five sapphires trimmed in silver bracelets. These he put in his homeboys' cars, each item by itself, and said to his homeboys, "Crank up the BMWs, the Benzes, and
He instructed the one in the lead: "When my brother Esau meets you and asks, to whom do you belong, and where are you going, and who owns all these animals in front of you?" Then you are to say, they belong to your servant Jacob. They are a gift sent to my lord Esau, and he is coming behind us,"	put space between the cars. Separate while delivering the gifts." Then to the first of his friends, saying, "When you see my brother, Esau, he's going to ask you who you hanging out with and who is the leader of your group. And whose are these ahead of you. Tell him that they belong to your homeboy
He also instructed the second, the third and all the others who followed the herds: You are to say the same thing to Esau when you meet him. And be sure to say, "Your servant Jacob is coming behind us. For he thought, I will pacify him with these gifts I am sending ahead of him, but he himself spent the night in the camp. (Genesis 32:13–21 NIV)	Jacob. It's a gift sent to you, my lord, Esau; he is behind us." So he buzzed the second leaders, the third, and all who followed in the dynamic cars, saying, "In this manner you rap with Esau when you meet him. And also say, 'Yo, your homeboy Jacob is behind us.' For he said, 'I want to make things right with the gifts that are dropped off before me; perhaps he will forgive me.'" So the gifts were delivered before him, but he himself lodged that night in the arcade room in the mall.

The dynamic translation gave the youth an opportunity to experience the text in a meaningful way because they had made it relevant to their experiences, and the whole congregation related to it. As a matter of fact, one of the young men in the youth group stated, "Dynamic translation made it relevant to past, present, and future. It took off years of studying it to find the meaning." This along with examples from the Parish Project Group members made the text relevant to a great deal of the body. Something in it drew everyone into the text and helped them identify with either Jacob or Esau and the need to forgive or to be forgiven.

The many examples that were given let them experience the text in ways with which they could connect, identify with the characters, and see the matter from both sides. With this in mind, the mission became presenting this opportunity to the congregation in the hope that they would begin the forgiving process by facing their hurts and confronting those issues that still remained painful for them.

This sermon became what Dow Edgerton would call the bread that would help to bring about the ultimate experience of recognizing the past and facing the old hurts that have caused parishioners to avoid each other, to avoid family members, and to live in fear of encountering someone from their past. If people are expected to change, change must be presented to them or fed to them regularly. If people are to experience forgiveness, it must be fed to them consistently.

In the text, Jacob had so feared Esau's revenge that he had not lived in peace for fear of having to encounter Esau someday. Esau on the other hand had moved on and was living his life fully. How many times does this happen today? People are so caught up in the past that they are unable to fully embrace the present or the future. In preaching and teaching forgiveness, the opportunity was presented for the congregation to face their past and from there move to the next step in the process of forgiveness—accepting what has happened.

SERMON 2

The Past: Embrace It

To forgive, we must move to the area of accepting the past for what it is and acknowledge the pain it caused; then it is possible to move into the future to which God is calling us. Paul said it well.

> Brethren, I do not count myself to have apprehended;
> but one thing I do, forgetting those things which are
> behind and reaching forward to those things which are
> ahead. (Philippians 3:12–13 NKJV)

Getting people to move forward requires the working of the Holy Spirit and their desire to do so.

How could we evoke in listeners the desire to experience forgiveness? First of all, the listeners have to be drawn into the sermon by an appeal to their core beliefs. In his book *Preaching as Celebration*, Frank Thomas introduced this as a part of the process of celebratory preaching.

> If the preacher would utilize emotional context and
> process in the preaching event, then the sermon must
> appeal to core belief. I believe human awareness
> involves three aspects of self: the cognitive, the
> emotive, and the intuitive. The cognitive is the
> faculty for reason and rational thought. The emotive
> is the basis for the arousal of feelings and affections.

> The intuitive is the capacity for direct knowing or learning beyond the conscious use of reasoning. Contained within the intuitive is the collection of core beliefs, broad principles for living shaped by cognitive, emotive, and intuitive evaluation of life and experience.[5]

People have deeply rooted life experiences that cause them to fear and hate and feel prejudice, unforgiveness, and anxiety. Preaching and teaching on an emotive and cognitive level and giving listeners the opportunity to apply this to their experiences will help them move beyond or to start overcoming these ingrained, painful experiences by helping them discover other options. This offers us the options of hope, trust, love, and forgiveness. To this end, the table must be set with plates that contain these options and served at every opportunity. How would we provide these options? The text used would be highly instrumental in this.

The text used for this sermon was the prodigal or lost son. In this text, the son took all that he had and squandered it on reckless living. Upon his return home, his father ran to him and embraced him—accepting him with unconditional love and forgiveness. No doubt the father had experienced hurt and disappointment at his son's departure and his son's poor choices, but his love for his son overshadowed everything else, and he showed his son unconditional love and forgiveness.

---

[5] Thomas, Frank A. *They Like to Never Quit Praisin' God: The Role of Celebration in Preaching.* New York: Pilgrim Press, 1997, 8–9.

FATHER AND DAUGHTER EMBRACING

What prevents us from forgiving? Often, it is unwillingness or the inability to express or really accept what has happened in our past as reality and then to work toward leaving it behind. We spend far too much time waiting for our past to catch up with us, far too much time looking in the rearview mirror, far too much time remembering how things used to be, and far too much time thinking this is where we belong when God is calling us to progress.

During an interview, a parishioner and member of the Parish Project Group shared her story with me. She said that when I first came to this parish and made changes in the leadership, she was moved out of her position as the coordinator of youth ministry. Initially, she felt great pain due to that and felt rejected. She was, however, able to get to a point that she realized she had a deeper calling to serve in the church. What she said she failed to recognize or acknowledge was that I had asked her to serve as the church lay leader. Her hurt feelings clouded her vision to see the greater responsibility and trust that was being placed in her.

This sermon connected with her; what was set before the prodigal son was an opportunity, and what was set before her was an opportunity as well. She could have gotten stuck in the past and failed to use the gifts and talents God had blessed her with because of a perceived injury. Her inability to not clearly understand the purpose or motive of the move prompted her pain and a lack of trust. However, keeping the focus of the ministry and open communication with the pastor allowed her to move past the pain and to embrace the ministry to which she was being assigned.

Many are not able to get past the pain, but she focused on the new task at hand in the midst of her pain, and that allowed room for the Holy Spirit to work in her just as the prodigal son's father's love for him overshadowed all the loss and disappointment. The love for ministry and open communication, which affords one the opportunity to freely express disagreement and gives freedom to do what God lays on one, opens the door to healing and wholeness.

I, the pastor, preacher, and teacher, recognized her gifts for higher leadership, but it was not until years later that I grasped the depth of the hurt she had experienced when she was removed from the youth ministry. Sometimes, the pastor, preacher, or teacher becomes the learner and experiences transformation in unexpected ways when he or she listens and opens the lines of communication. Change can be difficult, but it is also a blessing from God. It is a reminder that we are called to a ministry of reconciliation. Now, the topic was relevant to the congregation, and we could begin crafting a sermon that would speak to it in ways that would encourage the hearers to embrace the past no matter how painful it is.

Through this sermon, we hoped the congregation would learn that by embracing our old hurts and pain, we could experience healing and forgiveness and the love of family, friends, and God. That became the purpose statement. The task became painting a picture through the sermon of how that would look. That meant that the sermon would have to take into consideration how this text could be used to help the message achieve that.

The process became utilizing all age levels of the congregation to participate in a Bible study of the text. Then utilizing the Parish Project Group to provide relevant life experiences and illustrations along with the dynamic translation, the sermon was formed. As the preacher, my task was to bring order to all that information and present it in a celebratory sermon that would help stir up the desire in parishioners to embrace their past pain. They would be moved through the experiences of the people in the sermon and think about what that meant for them.

The sermon evolved into and incorporated the emotive, cognitive, and intuitive levels. We began with the life examples and dynamic translations. We set the table for all; I made the invitation; and we trusted the Holy Spirit to do the rest.

Preaching can bring about forgiveness, reconciliation, and transformation particularly when it contains a relevant message and true-to-life examples. In a dynamic translation, the scripture was given as a story of a young man who had taken the money his father had saved for his college education and lost it on bad investments and chasing an unrealistic dream, a contemporary version of the prodigal son's story. The following is the dynamic translation from sermon 2, The Past: Embrace It.

A man had two sons. Since they had been born, he had been putting money aside for their college education. The youngest son decided when he graduated from high school that he didn't want to go to college. He convinced his father to give him all the money he had saved for his college education and tried to get into the music industry and make lots of money. Well, after spending all the money on bad music deals, partying, and trying to live the life of a superstar, he found himself out on the street, homeless, and trying to get odd jobs to make a living. He has no college education, so no one was willing to hire him. He started running errands for drug dealers and risking going to jail all because he was too ashamed to go home and admit he had failed at his music career.

One day while trying to earn a quick dollar, he heard music and singing coming from a church on the corner, which was just like the one he had grown up in. He remembered that his father had been a musician in the church all his life and that it had brought him much joy. He remembered being in the choir himself and feeling good about that. He decided to go home and tell his father that he had been wrong to spend all his money so foolishly. If his father would have him back home, he would work his way through college and serve in the church when needed.

This story appealed to younger parishioners, but we wanted to make it relevant to older parishioners as well. We used a story from an episode of the *Andy Griffith Show* as an illustration that would be familiar to them.

In that episode, a man whom Andy had sent to prison was getting out of jail. He was coming to town and sent word to Andy that he wanted to see him. At first, Andy didn't think anything about it, but Barney made a big deal of it and told Andy that the man was probably gunning for him to exact revenge.

Barney made Goober and Gomer deputies, and even Aunt Bee and Opie started to get a little nervous. The man came to town and went to Andy's house carrying a long bag that looked like a shotgun could have been in it. As he was coming up the walk, Barney, Gomer, and Goober were panicking, and even Andy had become nervous. The man reached into the bag and pulled out a gift for Andy. He had come to thank him and to tell him that if he hadn't arrested him, his life would never have changed.[6] (Excerpt from Sermon 2: The Past: Embrace It

How do you know that you hit the mark with a sermon, that you fulfilled the purpose for having preached it? Your work is not done yet even though Sunday worship has passed and the sermon has been delivered. It is time to debrief, and that should include getting feedback from the Parish Project Group, the Bible study group, and any others involved in the sermon preparation process. Follow up with them, and reflect on the sermon together.

According to the Parish Project Group members, the sermon was well received by all age levels. The goal was to engage each member on a personal level and provide the opportunity for them to reflect on their past. The group reported that members were observed as they listened to the sermon. Many nodded in agreement when something seemed to touch them personally or caused them to think deeper. At times, there was complete silence, which indicated to the group that every ear was listening to an important message.

And that observed effect was confirmed. One member observed changes in a person with whom the person had had difficulty working; something had changed about that person, and they were interacting in a more positive way. It seemed that the sermon had evoked the emotive, cognitive, and intuitive responses in the listeners we had hoped for. This in turn caused reflection on their own lives to determine if in fact they were still carrying baggage from the past that needed to be embraced and dealt with.

How can this benefit an individual, a congregation, and a community? Preaching should encompass the present, examine the past, and provide direction for the future, and it involves teamwork. Those involved in the process feel ownership in it, which leads them to

---

[6] Excerpt from Sermon 2: The Past Embrace It.

be more open, honest, trusting, and willing to share their most sacred scars. It is in teamwork that community is revealed and connected to the text. The preacher, the teacher, learns the community's full narrative that is often hidden from sight or overlooked even when it is in plain sight.

The only way we can achieve healing and wholeness is by embracing the past and start letting it go.

SERMON 3
The Past: Kiss It Goodbye

On our journey toward forgiveness, reconciliation, and transformation, there comes a point that we need to let go of our past hurts and disappointments. In this sermon, I proposed that people would face the pain of their past and kiss it goodbye just as if they had company and kissed them goodbye after they had been there long enough. I wanted to challenge parishioners to no longer allow their past to cloud their vision of their future.

Why do we hold onto the past when it hurts so much? Many have made their pain a constant companion with which they have become familiar and comfortable; their pain has become a part of who they are. Living without the pain would be living an unfamiliar and new life, a challenge that might seem overwhelming for some. Our challenge is to let go of the pain we are carrying, lighten the load that we bear, and cast our cares on Jesus, for he cares for us.

Preaching transforms. When hearts are convicted, people can learn to live new lives. Preaching and teaching forgiveness can help people embrace new lives that allow them to be fully alive. The hymnist wrote, "And are we yet alive?" To be fully alive is to embrace each day with its promise of new wisdom, knowledge, experience, and the unknown that causes us to breathe deeply as we are refreshed by the mystery life holds. When we hold onto the old stuff of the past, we feel trapped in a reality that does not allow us to fully experience the breath of God. This is our present and our future. When we are locked in a painful past, we cannot fully comprehend or appreciate the future that God calls us to.

A perfect example of this would be having a bad experience on the job. As a result of bad experiences at work, people can hold themselves back from promotions because they put everything to the same test to prevent a recurrence of the pain. They begin to measure everything by that same tool. They tend to take their mistrust of authority or coworkers into every area of their career. Only when someone speaks openly and honestly with them will they be able to look at how they are holding themselves back from living up to their full potential.

Preaching and teaching forgiveness and reconciliation can open the eyes of those who are in need of being convicted and help them transform themselves. Preaching strips away the covering of sin and exposes it for what it really is. Then and only then can transformation take place and allow a difference to be made.

In this sermon, the metaphor used for leaving the past behind is Joseph kissing his brothers and forgiving them. It showed his willingness to help them during the famine they were going through.

Joseph exemplified God's forgiveness and began the process of release for his brothers and himself. When Joseph kissed his brothers, all the guilt and shame they had carried around started to fade. The touch of the one they had harmed began to restore them. They wanted to flee from his sight, but his touch, embrace, and kiss held them there; the baggage of the past was ready to be cast into the sea of forgetfulness and forgiveness.

I'm so glad that it didn't stop with Joseph. Jesus, betrayed, hurt, disappointed, persecuted, and killed, didn't let us flee from his sight.

Jesus embraced us and said, "Father, forgive them, for they do not know what they are doing" (Luke 23:34a NKJV)[7]

The brothers and Joseph alike were brought to a point of humility; they were in a position where God could use them. This was affirmed by the Parish Project Group. In their group response for this sermon, they stated that they felt the sermon had achieved its purpose—to move people to see the need to forgive and let go of the past so it would not affect their futures.

Further reflection by the Parish Project Group and me reinforced the idea that this project addressed a real need in a congregation. This complex and sensitive subject of forgiveness is at the heart of many issues that affect individuals, families, and communities. The question is, "How can they hear without a preacher?" (Romans 10:14c NKJV).

Employing the preaching as celebration style made the sermon effective. This was a sermon with deep purpose, and it needed to move people to action. We needed to reach deeply into the core of the hearers, where their dearest beliefs lay. Not only evoking emotion but impacting those core beliefs was the goal. In his book *They Like to Never Quit Praisin' God*, Frank Thomas wrote, "Celebrative design does not intend to move people for the sake of moving people; rather it intends to move people as part of the process of impacting core belief."[8] Using the celebratory style of preaching helps to take a delicate, painful issue and draw the listener into the story while exposing the pain. Then as the hearers are drawn in and see how their lives are mirrored in the scriptures and the contemporary illustrations, the options they have to resolve their situations are shared. Then the celebration begins that there is good news. No matter how difficult things are or have been, there is still hope.

[7] Except from Sermon 3: The Past: Kiss it Goodbye
[8] Thomas, *They Like to Never Quit Praisin' God*, 11.

Summary

> And how shall they preach, except they be sent?
> (Romans 10:15a NKJV)

Maybe God has placed you where you are at this time to help bring about healing. When we preach and teach forgiveness, we offer others the opportunity to have their eyes opened to the gospel of Jesus Christ. For people to engage in authentic relationships that allow them to experience God's love, forgiveness needs to take place. Letting unforgiveness go unchecked leads to the deterioration of our emotional, social, physical, and spiritual health. Issues will continue to tear at, plague, and hinder people as long as they are unresolved. Through preaching and teaching, these issues are brought out and options are offered for resolution. Forgiveness is the first step in the process; it is the catalyst for healing. When we forgive, we can take the next step—to reconciliation.

CHAPTER 2

RECONCILIATION

Now all things are of God, who has reconciled us to Himself through Jesus Christ, and has given us the ministry of reconciliation, that is, that God was in Christ reconciling the world to Himself, not imputing their trespasses to them, and has committed to us the word of reconciliation. (2 Corinthians 5:18–19 NKJV)

STATUE OF CHRIST

While preaching and teaching forgiveness and reconciliation lead to healing and wholeness that brings about transformation, the boldness and conviction in the delivery of the sermon is crucial in the impact it can have. For true impact, the teacher or preacher must believe what he or she is proclaiming.

What would be the benefit of forgiveness if no reconciliation took place? Without reconciliation, forgiveness is incomplete. If forgiveness was the end of the process, an opportunity to move to the next level of spiritual maturity and wholeness would be missed. Not being able to forgive breaks fellowship, and that hinders the ability of the body of Christ to build up God's kingdom. The task of preachers, teachers, and leaders becomes articulating that out of forgiveness comes the power that allows us, as Christians, to work together. This can take place only through reconciliation.

Reconciliation comes from the verb *reconcile*. According to *Webster's*, to reconcile is to restore to friendship or harmony, to settle or resolve differences, to make consistent or congruous, to cause to submit to or accept something unpleasant.[9]

When reconciliation takes place, ministry happens. Allowing God's grace to work in and through us gives us the strength and ability to work together toward a common goal—making disciples of Jesus Christ for the transformation of the world.

When a person, congregation, organization, community, group, or even a nation realizes the need for forgiveness and is open to communicating and accepting direction for reconciling their differences, they become open to the preaching, teaching, and facilitation of reconciliation and realize the power of working together, for it is the ministry to which we have been called.

What plays a major role in facilitating this is having a small group dedicated to working through this process and discussing biblical texts. This same process can be used to facilitate conversations that help bring reconciliation and healing in communities and serve national interests where we see polarization and economic divisions. This process takes time, but you will be amazed at the progress that can be made in a year

---

[9] *Merriam-Webster's Collegiate Dictionary.*

of this type of work as it causes people to realize the need for forgiveness to take place. Embodying that forgiveness becomes the focus.

Preaching and Teaching Reconciliation: The Power of Working Together

What would it look like to embody forgiveness? True forgiveness is active, not passive; it must be lived out in our daily lives. When we move past our hurts, betrayals, and disappointments, we begin to see the larger purpose to which God has called all Christians. How can we be effective kingdom builders if we cannot work together when our relationships fall short of our expectations for them? Addressing brokenness is not merely about spirituality. Reconciliation addresses the suffering and injury of those on the margins. Reconciliation helps us find our way to justice, and justice helps us find our way to peace.

Here's a story to consider. Someone who had been married for more than twenty years had an affair and asked his wife for a divorce; he planned to move in with his girlfriend. The wife was crushed; she had had no idea that this was coming. During the process of divorce, he became gravely ill and could not care for himself. His wife had moved on by that point and was in a new relationship. His supposed soulmate told him that his sickness was just too much for her to deal with.

The wife could have gone through with the divorce. She could have stayed with him and made him suffer for his betrayal of her. Or she could have nursed him back to health before deciding what she wanted to do after that.

What would you do in her situation? Her options called on her to give up something of herself, but two of them would have required her to become someone other than who she was. She might have gotten revenge, but she would not have ended up reconciled to herself.

Forgiveness and reconciliation are not just for the other person; they are also for us.

Sometimes, we give others too much power over us when we carry the hurt and pain around. We almost seem to live for it. In this case, the rejected spouse tried to do the right thing, but it was hard; she did inflict some pain on him while caring for him because he was at first less than grateful for her help. They were becoming people who were not proud of whom they had become. They forgave each other and reconciled.

Did they live happily ever after? Absolutely. Just not together. They found the power of working together, but that didn't mean that their original relationship was restored; they did, however, learn to live in peace and harmony, and that was important if they wanted to heal.

It is in us to want to do the right thing, but sometimes, things cause us to lose ourselves and become outraged and even bitter. When we can remember who we are and whose we are, our hardened hearts can become sincere and we can genuinely hope for good for all.

Preaching and teaching that call us to accountability help us prepare the ground for the work needed to be done. We have to hear a biblical text that calls us to see ourselves in the story, examine the characters in the story, and see how we identify with them. The following are three sermons that helped us do this. These sermons call us to confront the physical and metaphorical walls that have been erected to protect us from those we fear or who have brought us pain in the past.

For this work, we selected the following three texts to be used in three sermons (which can be found in their entirety in appendix B) to address the needs of our community of faith and our community as a whole.

- Acts 2:42–47 With a Sincere Heart
- 2 Corinthians 5:16–21 It's a Ministry
- Nehemiah 1:3–6 The Power of Working Together

Here, the biblical texts were used to help draw listeners into the stories so that they could see and experience the power of God's Word and how it could help people understand the need to reconcile their differences for their own good as well as the good of the community.

SERMON 1
With a Sincere Heart

What a grand future the Church has if we could learn to work together. The church is not just for us today, but for our children's children and their children. It is for generations to come until Jesus returns. And so, we learn to work together for the building of God's Kingdom. If we could just learn to put aside our differences, what a bold and bright light the Church would be to the world. Well how do we come to a place of working together in the power of the Holy Spirit? It is with a sincere heart—a heart of repentance and sorrow for poor decisions, disagreements, and lack of faith in God[10].

When we can reconcile our differences, we can begin to work together, but that is easier said than done; it takes "heart" work and discipline. We need sincere hearts and the Holy Spirit to empower us to reconcile our differences, and we have to genuinely desire reconciliation. This will have to be illustrated in such a way that the listeners are moved to reconcile. This is where the small group and Bible study groups came in. In our case, they were able to share the stories that would connect to the text and be incorporated in the sermon.

---

[10] Excerpt from Sermon 1: With A Sincere Heart

One of the stories used physical fitness and exercise as an analogy for a spiritual fitness program. A parishioner stated that having a sincere heart to serve required spiritual fitness and discipline. To embody forgiveness and move to reconciliation, we must be intentional about doing the work required. This can lead to living lives of forgiveness and reconciliation and thus move past the painful issues and work together.

The text used to illustrate the points in this sermon was Acts 2:42–47. The task was to take the congregation into the church in Acts 2 and help them realize that there was great power in being able to reconcile differences for the sake of the gospel. People walking in harmony and unity are powerful witnesses who can lead others to Christ. However, if we do not realize that there is great benefit in working through differences, we will miss out on walking fully in God's calling.

The process begins with studying the biblical text. Open discussion here can bring out some personal stories that open the door for sharing. The shared stories become illustrations that can be used in the sermon to address some unresolved issues.

The next step is coming up with relevant illustrations with which hearers can identify. For this group, follow-up after the sermon indicated that the purpose had been achieved effectively. This feedback was good, but what happened in the days that followed made it even more worthwhile.

Later that evening during a small-group disciple Bible study, the sermon came up; the group was on fire from the message. This confirmed what I had believed—that there was a need to address forgiveness and reconciliation. Additionally, an encounter with a member later in the week also revealed a struggle with forgiving. This parishioner stated, "I realized from the sermon that I needed to forgive." The part of the message on not sitting down on God or giving up all hope seemed to have reached this parishioner.

Preaching and teaching forgiveness to lead to transformation was the foundation of this project. However, the styles and techniques used for delivery are crucial to the impact the sermons have on the hearers. Here is what helped to make the difference. I had digested the text. I walked around with it. I allowed it to grab me. Having read *The Jazz of Preaching: How to Preach with Freedom and Joy* by Kirk Byron Jones, I knew that delivering a sermon in a natural way and drawing listeners into it could make a great impact on them. Because of my connection with the text, it was in mind, heart, and spirit. I knew it. Not having to deliver it verbatim from a manuscript freed me to reach into my hearers' hearts and bring them into the text. They were able to look at themselves without intimidation or judgment. Rather than shut down or tune the preacher out, they tuned in because they heard something that resembled situations they had experienced or were going through.

Using what I had learned from Dr. Jones, I observed what was going on in the congregation and brought that into the moment. The songs we sang, the liturgy that had been read, and any prayers or testimonies that had been offered allowed me to draw in the listeners to the sermon in a meaningful way. They confirmed that they felt more connected to the sermon than they had been. That led to some repenting, others opening the door of communication, and others reaching out to begin a dialogue that should have taken place a long time ago. To God be the glory!

SERMON 2

It's a Ministry

Christ died so that our sins would be forgiven and that we would be reconciled to God; therefore, we should be reconciled to one another. This ministry of Christ is our ministry too. Reconciliation is a ministry at the heart of God's love for humanity and all God's creation. When we forgive others, that releases them from owing us anything, and we model Christ in our lives. Forgiveness changes us and moves us to a place of witnessing to others by being ambassadors or representatives of reconciliation through Christ.

The proposal for this sermon was this.

> It is my belief that unless Christians are willing and intentional about working through their differences, they cannot be in ministry with a sincere heart. I propose that the hearer will gain a clearer understanding of Christ's ministry of reconciliation and our need to be in a ministry of reconciliation. And as a result experience and live out God's love in action, deed and word every day.

Getting listeners to engage in reconciliation was one goal of the sermon. I wanted to use stories and illustrations that would touch them while allowing for their personal issues to remain anonymous. Using stories that they offered helped to connect the congregation to their personal experiences.

The preacher's challenge is to remember that congregations are made up of family in rural, suburban, and urban areas, so appealing to their personal experiences has a greater impact when the preaching and teaching incorporates stories and illustrations without making known who the people in the story are.

Utilizing the creative, imaginative storytelling method taught in the *Jazz of Preaching*, I wove these stories into the sermon to make them more effective. They propelled the text in the way I believe God intended. What made the difference was that I had read, digested, and reviewed the stories throughout the week; I had internalized them by the time I gave the sermon. The authenticity of the stories was transformational even though no names were mentioned.

The story about Paco and his father, who had not spoken to each other in many years, touched the hearts of many of my parishioners. (See appendix B.) After reading a note placed in the personal ads to Paco in a newspaper in Spain, hundreds of young men responding to the offer of reconciliation made by the father. Paco is a common name in Spain, and obviously, more than one young man had experienced the heartache of not having had a relationship with their father. One member of the Parish Project Group said, "It made me realize that so many people have the same problem. That was powerful." This rang true in our own group as a young adult said that he took that story personally. He had given up hope on the situation between him and his father, but the story of Paco made him realize that there is always hope.

The small group believed that being an ambassador is an important role. We cannot allow ourselves to be sidetracked; we must stay true to the ministry to which God has called us. Being in ministry, true ministry, involves reconciliation. If we are unwilling to forgive and work through our differences, we cannot engage in authentic, fruitful ministry. In fact, it makes maintaining any relationship extremely difficult.

SERMON 3

The Power of Working Together

Have you ever been in a position of being comfortable and safe, yet all around you there is work to be done for God's Kingdom? Nehemiah was in such a position. When we meet him he is wearing a robe of royalty. He is the King's cupbearer. Even though he was in a position of power, his heart beat for the people in Israel; he was a Hebrew in Persia. When word reached him concerning the condition of Jerusalem and the people, Nehemiah invited God to use him.[11]

Nehemiah prayed and then traded his robe for coveralls and went to work. This was at the heart of reconciliation: the power of working together. When we reconcile our differences, we can work together to accomplish great tasks for the greater good. We are able to accomplish what God deems important. Broken relationships are divisive. Division among those in a family, church, organization, community, government, or nation can hinder many people's ability to work together for their own good or the good of others.

The light of the church does not shine when there is brokenness, division, and strife. We cannot let our relationships lie in ruin and stall our ministry while the world is in need of seeing the light of Christ. The ability to see the bigger picture and the great ends to which God is leading us allows us to move forward intentionally to work together.

Using the analogy of an earthquake, the sermon paints a picture of what it would be like for people who had not seen eye to eye in the past to work together for a common cause. In this case, a highway had been destroyed by a quake, and that stopped a community from getting medical assistance; they had to rebuild it regardless of their races, political beliefs, and other differences. The power of working together in this case came from being a genuine part of the community. When we rise above our differences and see our common needs, we can reconcile those differences and work together.

None of us can make it alone; we need each other. The point of this message is that when people realize the benefit of working together, what a joy that can be. Then we are able to accomplish together far greater things than we could as individuals.

---

[11] Excerpt from Sermon 3: The Power of Working Together.

Summary

The goal of these sermons and the Bible studies that led to them was to move beyond forgiveness into reconciliation and the next step—working together. This is where the power of the gospel is embodied and lived out. When believers can work side by side with those with whom they have had disagreements, fallouts, and all types of conflict, the power of the gospel is unleashed and great work takes place.

Working together is not the end of the process, however; something far more wonderful takes place. When we can offer and receive forgiveness, we are forever changed. Transformation takes place. We can begin to resemble Christ.

CHAPTER 3

TRANSFORMATION

Do not conform any longer to the pattern of this world, but be transformed by the renewing of your mind. Then you will be able to test and approve what God's will is—his good pleasing and perfect will. (Romans 12:2 NIV)

A caterpillar goes into a cocoon a worm and emerges a beautiful butterfly. A metamorphosis occurs in the cocoon. Just like butterflies, we can undergo metamorphoses and become beautiful creations full of joy and life. What then does it mean to be transformed?

COCOON

When we are transformed, we are changed from the inside out, refashioned into something different from what we were originally.

Up to this point, the focus has been on preaching and teaching forgiveness and reconciliation to bring about healing and wholeness. Bible studies and sermons have been focused on the need to acknowledge the past, accept it for what it is, and move on. These following two sermons are a culmination of this process.

When we are forgiven and when we forgive, we are transformed, and that leads to wholeness. When we are transformed, our minds are renewed and we are recreated into what God wants us to be.

Transformation comes when we have made a complete change of the old and become totally new. To move from the issues of the past that have caused pain and hurt for so long and to become whole, we must change our way of thinking. Old thoughts of pain, hurt, and disappointment have to be replaced with new insights, new thoughts, and divine wisdom. We need the transforming power of the Holy Spirit.

SERMON 1

Being Transformed

> Do not be conformed any longer to this world, but
> be transformed through the renewing of your minds.
> (Romans 12:2a NRSV)

Transformation is an act. When someone starts treating us differently, we realize that they have been transformed. Someone who has been transformed is different on the inside.

Unforgiveness affects us on different levels. There is the individual level, and there is the level where we are affected as a church, as a community, and as a society. Preaching and teaching forgiveness can bring about transformation that affects society; it can bring about change in the world.

All hurt and injury is not caused by people we know or by those with whom we are affiliated. Some hurts come from sources that are difficult to put a face on. They are the so-called powers that be. They are those issues such as racism, classism, and other isms and prejudices that cause us to treat each other differently. Injustice causes hurt and pain that bring about unforgiveness. Preaching to address issues in society helps heal brokenness caused by institutional, systemic transgressions. Preaching as a social act can bring about transformation in society. This sermon used that concept very effectively by taking the current issue of the day involving the Jenna Six and incorporating it into the message by pointing to local issues of the same type. It is important to address these issues because they can cause generations of pain.

Many in minority communities still remember the pain of racism that was inflicted upon blacks for many, many years. Native Americans suffer from generational trauma because of the violence and losses they suffered. Currently, there is a great divide in our country concerning immigrants and persons who come to this country seeking a better way of life. Families are separated and children are left to fend for themselves as mothers and fathers are detained or deported. An alarming number of men and women of color are dying at the very hands of those who swore an oath to protect and serve them. Young black men are more likely to go to prison than to college. Our nation today is extremely polarized. Many of us live between the right and the left and the red and the blue, yet there is only a sense of the extremes. Many are hurting because the issues at the core of the problem are not being addressed and often not even acknowledged. When these issues are not addressed, healing cannot take place, society cannot function as a whole, and no one is able to enjoy peace of mind.

This sermon offered some ways that transformation can take place as a result of forgiveness and reconciliation. One way is for us to gather at the table of grace to address the causes of pain, hurt, and disappointment. Another way is for us to unmask the powers that be by speaking truth and acknowledging that it exists. When we are willing to see ourselves as we are, then and only then can we let go of our hurt, bitterness, and emotional baggage and allow joy to return to our lives, community, church, and nation. When we find laughter again, we have a different perception of life. This is important as restoration can begin to take place. Through the Word of God and the power of the Holy Spirit, our minds and hearts are open to be changed. "A renewed mind is essential to the discernment of God's will and the transformation of life."[12]

This sermon used the illustration of the popular movie *The Transformers*. The Transformers are superheroes. We can all identify with superheroes from our childhood and youth. Superheroes fight for

---

[12] *The Interpreter's Study Bible*, volume 9. Nashville: Abingdon Press, 2003.

the good of all often sacrificing their well-being for that of others. They often end up helping their archenemies—Yes, those who try to harm them end up being rescued by the superheroes. The Transformers can change their appearance when fighting evil, and we too can undergo changes after we put aside whatever we hold against others and work to help them despite our differences. In doing so, we and they are humbled and transformed.

SERMON 2

An Encounter with God ...
An Encounter with Forgiveness

When we come face to face with God, we are never the same again. Each time we experience the mercy and the grace of God, we encounter God. That is exactly what happened with Paul on the road to Damascus. As he encountered the risen Savior, his life was changed and he began to see things in a new light; that encounter transformed him.

The task for this sermon was to articulate how that would look today. The Parish Project Group was extremely helpful in providing real-life illustrations of transformation that had taken place and people who were changed in such a way that it was visible for all to see.

One illustration was based on the life of George Wallace, a former governor of Alabama. Wallace had become a champion for segregation who had vowed to uphold the laws that kept African-Americans and white people separate as long as he was standing. While making a bid for the presidency, Wallace was left crippled by a bullet from an assassination attempt. He lived the remainder of his life in a wheelchair. He changed his stance on civil rights and became a champion of equal rights.

When he ran for governor of Alabama again, he was elected. His greatest supporters were African-Americans. The story was so valuable in this sermon because it was a true story pulled from the history of civil rights in this country and because it showed how a great transformation could take place in an individual and bring about healing to the masses.

Another illustration was of a United Methodist missionary's experience in Vietnam during a worship service. A man with just one arm gave his testimony of how God had touched his life. He told the story of how he had been a soldier in the Vietnam War who had been captured. During an attempt to escape from prison, a Vietnamese soldier shot his arm off in retaliation for his escape attempt. A man next to him stood and said, "I am that man." Because of the forgiveness that had taken place, the lives of both of these men had been changed. The first man experienced it when he forgave the one who had shot his arm off, and the second when he experienced the forgiveness of this man and the mercy and the grace of God. This sermon was preached on Veteran's Day, and the fact that it was a true story of transformation powerfully illustrated that when we can forgive and reconcile, we can experience healing and wholeness. We can have the joy of life back that we once knew.

This is what happened with Paul when he was blinded by the light of the love of the one he was persecuting. It is often beyond our comprehension and understanding how we can be forgiven for some things we have done. We struggle with forgiving ourselves. This sermon brought full circle the initial proposal for this book. It is not always the one injured who has difficulty in forgiving and letting go; at times, the problem is the unwillingness of the one who has caused injury to accept forgiveness.

Real transformation is possible when it is taught. Faithful teaching and preaching on the value of forgiveness and reconciliation can and will lead to transformation that brings about healing and wholeness.

Summary

Unforgiveness can wreak havoc in our lives. Holding onto and internalizing things that have caused us pain and hurt bring about physical, emotional, mental, social, and spiritual illness. The inability to unpack and process what is hurting inside can manifest itself in ways that are damaging to our physical health; ulcers, cancer, and other ailments can develop from internalizing issues that are too painful to discuss. Relationships can suffer, families can be destroyed, job performance can be affected, and our ability to pray and to have communion with God can be hindered when we are unable to live free of unforgiveness.

And so the conversation has to start somewhere. If it cannot start with the parties involved, it has to come from other sources. Preaching and teaching can start that reflection and open the door for those conversations and begin the healing process. I believe that I have been called to start that reflection, to open the door for that conversation, and to help facilitate the dialogue.

CHAPTER 4

THE CONGREGATION'S/ COMMUNITY'S RESPONSE

A key component to the success of this process is the involvement of the family, congregation, or community. The experiences shared and the feedback given will be invaluable. These responses will help you realize the impact the work you are doing is having.

The congregation's response is based on their experience of the sermons on forgiveness, reconciliation, and transformation. This book includes quotes and statements concerning the congregation's response to particular sermons. Lives are being transformed. We were more open to communication and working together than we had been. People seemed to be more willing to acknowledge when they were wrong, to explain misunderstandings, and to invite dialogue instead of breaking off fellowship. This work is the culmination of the effect preaching and teaching forgiveness and reconciliation have had on this parish as a whole. You can do this same work in your own context or area of ministry.

Interviews were conducted with members of the congregation. A broad representation of the parish was included in this process. All age levels, regular and irregular attendees, leaders, and others had the opportunity to have their input taken into consideration. The pastor and the Parish Project Group came up with the questions; they were incorporated from various age levels to include in the interviews. They were asked what types of questions they would use to evaluate sermons to determine the *effect* of, the *growth* of, and the *transformation* of the hearers in interviews in a particular age level. These were compiled in an interview questionnaire. The results of the interviews are on the following pages.

Compilation of Interview Results

Overwhelmingly, parishioners responded to the sermons in a positive way. Here are the results of fifty interviews.

Statistical Information

- Regularly attend worship   39
- Not so regularly attend worship   2
- Occasionally attend worship   3
- Attend Bible study   27
- Attend Sunday school   11
- Attend other ministries   13

Interview Questions

Describe any changes you have noted in the pastor's preaching. (Check as many as apply.)

- More powerful   29
- More interesting   22
- More energetic   22
- More colorful   8

Has the preaching resulted in any change in your deeply held beliefs?

- Definitely   34
- Somewhat   16
- Not at all   0

How often can you apply the lessons in the sermon to your daily life?

- Often   33
- Sometimes   16
- Rarely   1
- Never   0

After hearing the sermon, you were moved to

- Mend a broken relationship   18
- Speak to someone   16
- Apologize   12
- Other actions   5
- Not moved at all   0

Do you think the purpose of the sermon was achieved?

- Definitely   41
- Somewhat   9
- Not at all   0

Did the pastor bring the scripture to life? Were you able to relate the subject to the scripture and to your daily life?

- Definitely   39
- Somewhat   11
- Not at all   0

CHAPTER 5

THE PREACHER'S EXPERIENCE

Preaching and teaching forgiveness and reconciliation transformed me as well as my parish. I believe that as a result of this project, my preaching has changed as have I.

I opened myself to the assistance of others for the formation and evaluation of my sermons. There has been preaching in the community, by the community, with the community, through the community, and ultimately to the community. This has called for me to stretch myself and allow the congregation to become part owners in sermons by providing feedback in group sessions and one-on-one interviews. This is a humbling experience to say the least, but it is a wonderful opportunity for growth. After all, preaching is not for the preacher alone; it should involve the congregation. Therefore, their input has been and will continue to be a valuable resource.

HANDS ON TREE

Second, due to this preaching project, I have taken courses that have taken my preaching to a new level. As this project progressed, I employed what I learned in the courses. I have also shared what I have learned with the Parish Project Group. Three of the courses I have used particularly are Preaching as Celebration, The Jazz of Preaching, and Preaching as a Social Act; they contain effective ways of delivering sermons and have helped me grow in my preaching.

I have more boldness and confidence when preaching due to the techniques I have learned and taught, and I trust myself to be open to tell my story along with the congregation's story. The Parish Project Group has entrusted me with their stories, and the Holy Spirit has incorporated our stories in God's story, and the power of the gospel has been unleashed.

When I read the text, digest it, and carry it with me throughout the week in meditation, it takes hold of me and I become part of the story. That makes its delivery much more challenging for me but much more interesting for the parishioners. This has been affirmed in the interviews we conducted. Parishioners have stated that my preaching is more powerful, interesting, and energetic. According to the interviews, they have seen the conviction with which I have preached, and that has helped the sermons hit their marks.

CONCLUSION

Preaching and teaching forgiveness and reconciliation to bring about transformation, healing, and wholeness in the church body is the focus of this book, but great merit has been and can be realized in the lives of individuals and families in and outside the church.

Church leaders are learning to work together for the benefit of the ministry God has entrusted to them. Family members who have not spoken for years can begin to have dialogue. Divorced parents come to realize that holding onto the pain of the past allows the dysfunction of the broken relationship to predominate in the lives of their children. Yes, progress can be made, but it will be ongoing.

I have been transformed. James talked about being doers of the Word, not just hearers of it. While preaching and teaching forgiveness and reconciliation in the parish, I was reminded of my own painful experience of unforgiveness I needed to reconcile with. I was challenged to become transparent and to share my story with the congregation. We strive to be authentic. I shared my story of how my father's unfulfilled promises to me broke the bond of trust we once had had. His desire to have a relationship with his grandchildren led me to be protective of them; I did not want them to experience the pain I had felt from disappointment brought on by broken promises. These unkept promises had become painful unresolved memories.

Being in ministry caused me to confront the grace of God in my life and the realization that Christians are called to the ministry of reconciliation. In spite of the pain I had experienced, my challenge was to forgive and let go of that pain and move on. My transformation came when I allowed my father to have a relationship with his grandchildren, and he and I have grown closer.

When we experience God's grace and understand forgiveness, then and only then will we be able to begin the process. The conversation has to start somewhere. If those involved cannot begin to work things out on their own, something has to evoke a response. Therefore, preaching and teaching forgiveness and reconciliation can transform lives and bring about healing and wholeness.

The Past, Face It

Text: Genesis 32:13–21

Key Verse: Genesis 32:20b

> For he thought, I may appease him with the present that goes ahead of me, and afterwards I shall see his face, perhaps he will accept me. (Genesis 32:20b NRSV)

Traditional Reading	Dynamic Translation
He spent the night there, and from what he had with him he selected a gift for his brother Esau: two hundred female goats and twenty male goats, two hundred ewes and twenty rams, Thirty female camels with their young, forty cows and ten bulls, and twenty female donkeys and ten male donkeys. He put them in the care of his servants, each herd by itself, and said to his servants, "Go ahead of me, and keep some space between the herds."	In the darkness of the midnight hour and from his store at the mall, Jacob selected gifts for his brother. One beautiful gold cross and three silver keys, two pairs of Timberlands, four pairs of Jordans, twenty SpongeBob SquarePants shirts, two pairs of Air Force Ones, two Tommy shirts, and five sapphires trimmed in silver bracelets. These he put in his homeboys' cars, each item by itself, and said to his homeboys, "Crank up the BMWs and the Benzes and put space between the cars, separate while delivering the gifts." Then to the first
He instructed the one in the lead: "When my brother Esau meets you and asks, to whom do you belong, and where are you going, and who owns all these animals in front of you?" Then you are	of his friends, saying, "When you see my brother Esau, he's going to ask you, 'Who you hanging out wit? And who is

to say, they belong to your servant Jacob. They are a gift sent to my lord Esau, and he is coming behind us,"

. He also instructed the second, the third and all the others who followed the herds: You are to say the same thing to Esau when you meet him. And be sure to say, "Your servant Jacob is coming behind us. For he thought, I will pacify him with these gifts I am sending ahead of him, but he himself spent the night in the camp. (Genesis 32:13–21 NIV)

the leader of your group? And whose are these ahead of you?' Tell him that they belong to your homeboy Jacob. It's a gift sent to you my lord Esau; he is behind us." So he buzzed the second leaders, the third, and all who followed in the dynamic cars, saying, "In this manner you rap with Esau when you meet him. And also say, 'Yo, your homeboy Jacob is behind us.' For he said, 'I want to make things right with the gifts that are dropped off before me; perhaps he will forgive me.'" So the gifts were delivered before him, but he himself lodged that night in the arcade room in the mall.

Let us reason together with the subject The Past: Face It. What joy, happiness, pain, loneliness, or disappointments of the past are you fearing this moment? Maybe it's the fear of unforgiveness for that wayward child, the one with the drug problem you tried to help, but he kept deceiving everyone in the family. You remember the family getting together to decide to send him away for help, but he left and found help and has rebuilt his life. Now he is afraid to return to his family because of the things he had done and said. He didn't know that the family had healed and some had actually forgotten and forgiven him for the things he did while he was under the influence of drugs.

Have you been wronged or harmed and responded, "I'm going to get even if it's the last thing I do"? For example, you have always wanted a particular position because you thought you could do a better job than the person in the position was doing, but the position was given to someone else. What do you do now, support that new person in his role or become a thorn in his side?

What keeps you from reconciling with family and friends? Perhaps you are in a dispute with a family member because of his or her handling of the finances of a departed loved one. As a result, you have not spoken to that person in a long time. The situation is made worse because there is physical as well as emotional distance between you and the loved one. What can you do? You can face the past.

Have you ever been on the street or in a store and seen someone from your past whom you would rather not meet up with? It might be someone you made fun of in school, or someone who had hurt your feelings badly. Maybe you have been avoiding people who live in your community whose children go to school with your children, and you may even attend the same church. The chances are greater that you did something to offend the other person if you are trying to avoid them. It may have been twenty, ten, or five years ago or maybe last year. No matter the time frame, you fear that one day, you will have to encounter your past.

In our text, for twenty years, Jacob had feared the day he would encounter his brother Esau. Jacob had fled Canaan having deceived his father, Isaac, and having robbed Esau of the all-important paternal blessing. Isaac had been rendered vulnerable by old age and had bad eyesight. All it took to make Isaac think that Jacob was Esau was a little musk, a little goat fur, and the willingness to tell a bold-faced lie. It worked of course. Jacob got the blessing, but he lost his home in the bargain.

Esau's anger was real, so before Rebekah's elder son could turn her beloved younger son into chopped-up meat, Rebekah sent Jacob packing. Jacob got the blessing because of his manipulation and his deception, but he had no peace.

So Jacob was coming home wondering when he would be held accountable. I imagine Jacob pacing like a general in a war room. He has maps on the wall and diagrams rolled out on a table. Can you see him walking around like he's done nothing wrong or has no fear, showing power in his flesh appearance?

Jacob spat out orders to his soldiers and hired hands. "Okay, we'll divide the clan into two groups. If one gets attacked, the other at least can survive by outflanking Esau while he's distracted by the battle."

A servant came from the field with some intelligence. "My lord, we've scouted up ahead. Esau is heading straight this way with an army of no less than four hundred!"

Jacob was shaking in fear of his past. "Now it's time to pray!" he shouted. He went before God in prayer thanking him for his kindness and mercies in enriching him in recent years but also recruiting his assistance in the conflict. It seemed as if he were saying, "Don't forget, O God, that you gave me a kind of blank-check promise back at Bethel years ago. You said you'd protect and prosper me, remember? Well, I'm cashing the check! Save me from Esau's anger!"

Having now prayed, it was back to the war room for General Jacob. He called in five of his best herdsmen, assigned each of them to take a herd of animals, and then to proceed in staggered formation toward Esau. "When you see Esau, tell him that I am coming along too, but that in the meanwhile, this herd of cattle is a gift from me to him." Jacob very cleverly released these five groups so that it would work out that for the better part of a day, Esau would receive yet another gift about once every hour or so. The idea seems to have been that he would steadily bombard Esau with goodness and so in this way, hopefully, chip away at any lingering anger Esau may have been harboring[13]

Jacob hoped the gifts would make Esau friendly, so Esau would be glad to see him when they met. The past can do two things for

---

[13] https://yardley.cs.calvin.edu/hoezee/topics/genesis/genesis32.html, by Scott Hoezee.

you. It can be a source of learning and experience, or it can be a heavy burden that holds you back from your fullness of life. How do you shake it? Lessons are learned by understanding Jacob's past and confronting our past. All the time that Jacob was working for his father-in-law, he worried about Esau. When he left there a wealthy man with wives, children, servants, and livestock, he still worried about Esau.

Check this out! He worried for nothing. Esau had let it go. Esau had learned from his mistakes and was living his life in fullness. Did you get that? Jacob was still wrestling with who he was, and wrestling with God, but Esau had forgotten the whole thing. He had forgiven Jacob. He had embraced his past, had learned from it, and had moved on. He just wanted to see his brother again. God had provided for Esau; he had wives, children, servants, and livestock just like Jacob did. Esau was living and enjoying life.

Some of us have forgotten what it's like to be happy and joyful because we are carrying around stuff from ten, fifteen, and even twenty years ago, stuff that happened, but we can't even remember all the details. Nonetheless, we hold onto the hard feelings. Some of those who were involved have forgotten what had happened. Some have gone on to be with the Lord. But we're still worrying about stuff that we should have let go a long time ago. Some of us can't let go because we know that what we had done was wrong. If that's the case, we need to face our past.

Some of us can't let go because we can't bring ourselves to communicate with the other people involved. If that's the case, we need to face our past.

Some of us can't let go because we've gotten so attached to the pain, bitterness, and hard feelings that letting go would leave us feeling empty. We really need to face our past.

There is good news today! You don't have to continue to beat yourself up. You don't have to continue to drag all that mess around behind you for the next twenty years. God, through His Son Jesus, has given us grace we can share with each other, grace that will make the twenty years that we may have lost be restored as we look forward to twenty new years. With God, there is always a chance for a fresh start.

Now is the time as we celebrate 139 years. I'm so glad that the God I serve is a gracious God. Look where he has brought you from. He brought those who came before you from gathering in a small group under a brush arbor to having a little wooden church building. Later building a bigger church, and after many years bricking that building, and then building this church.

Now is the time. The past … Face it. We don't have to run from our past. We should embrace it and experience the love that was there all the time. Now is the time. Face it. Don't miss the joy of the Lord because of stubbornness, pride, or fear. God has given us the blessing he had promised to those generations and generations before us, and we can't take that lightly; we must hold onto it.

What will be your next step? Looking back over the 139 years, how wonderful would it be to take all of your old hurts, resentment, anger, bitterness, unforgiveness, mistrust, and leave it at the altar today and then look forward to where God is taking us. Let's leave the past where it best belongs … in the past.

The Past: Embrace It
Text: Luke 15:11–20
Key Verse: Luke 15:20

> So he got up and went to his father. But while he was still a long way off, his father saw him and was filled with compassion for him; he ran to his son, threw his arms around him and kissed him. (Luke 15:20 NIV)

Jesus continued: "There was a man who had two sons. The younger one said to his father, 'Father, give me my share of the estate.' So he divided his property between them. Not long after that, the younger son got together all he had, set off for a distant country and there squandered his wealth in wild living. After he had spent everything, there was a severe famine in that whole country, and he began to be in need. So he went and hired himself out to a citizen of that country, who sent him to his fields to feed pigs. He longed to fill his stomach with the pods that the pigs were eating, but no one gave him anything. When he came to his senses, he said, 'How many of my father's hired servants have food to spare, and here I am starving to death! I will set out and go back to my father and say to him: Father, I have sinned against heaven and against you. I am no longer worthy to be called your son; make me like one of your hired servants.' So he got up and went to his father. But while he was still a long way off, his father saw him and was filled with compassion for him; he ran to his son, threw his arms around him and kissed him." (Luke 15:11–20 NIV)

This is the second of three sermons on forgiveness. The first message was The Past: Face It. We learned that by facing our past, we can get at the heart of the issues that cause us pain and keep us from giving and receiving forgiveness. We learned that our past can be a source of learning instead of a hindrance to our future. In addition, we learned that holding onto old hurts can strip our lives of the peace God desires for us.

The last time, we talked about some people from your past whom you may have hurt or offended or who may have hurt or offended you. Whatever the case may be, all of a sudden, you look up and there they are. They are too close to you for you to get out of the way. The last thing you want is for them to see you. Too late. They've recognized you, and they're coming over to you. You search for the words to say, but before you can say anything, they grab you by the hand and give you a big hug. There you are standing with your mouth open wondering what to say.

The last time you had an encounter with them, you were sure that they would never speak to you again. Now, here they are embracing you. You stumble over your words trying to offer an apology, but they don't seem to understand what you're talking about. When you finally get it out, they say, "Oh that! I let go of that a long time ago" or "We were just kids back then" or "Things turned out just the way they should have." The past … Embrace it.

A man had two sons. Since they were born, he had been putting money aside for their college education. The youngest son decided at graduation that he didn't want to go to college, so he convinced his father to give him the money he had intended for his college expenses and went to the city, where he thought he would get into the music industry and make lots of money.

Well, after spending all the money he had on bad music deals, partying, and trying to live the life of a superstar, he found himself running errands for drug dealers and risking going to jail all because he was too ashamed to go home and tell his father that he had failed at his music career.

One day on a drug drop, he heard music and singing coming from a church on the corner. The church reminded him of the one he had attended growing up. He remembered that his father had been a musician in the church all his life, and it seemed to bring him so much joy. He looked back and remembered those days that he had been in the church choir and how he sometimes helped out with the music. He remembered that it had made him feel good too. He made up his mind to tell his father that he was wrong to spend his college money so foolishly. If his father would have him back home, he would work his way through college and serve in the church when needed. The past … Embrace it.

Life is full of surprises. There are fun surprises like birthday parties and Christmas gifts. There are also the surprises of the past that you experience that reveal something about who you are and who your God is. Those are the kind of surprises that Jesus gave to people in his parables. When he told a parable, it was to answer a question or to deal with an attitude. Most of the parables had surprise endings that drove right into the heart of the issue and to the heart of the individuals listening.[14]

In our text, this young man doubted the capability and goodness of his father. He thought he could do a better job of managing his life than his father could. This is a perfect picture of our natural heart, which resists the rule of God in our lives. We want to be independent. Here are two questions we need to ask ourselves.

The first is, How am I being independent? It could be with your finances, trusting in lottery tickets instead of trusting in your relationship with God. It could be a sinful habit and looking for happiness in other things instead of relying on God. We cling to things that we do well or things we think are meeting our needs or making life work, and we refuse to depend on God and let him meet our needs.

The second is, Why am I being independent? I think it is because we doubt the goodness of God. I think that is the reason the son left.

---

[14] https://bible.org/seriespage/12-lost-sheep-coins-and-sons

He doubted the goodness of his father, and he thought he could handle life better on his own.

The son squandered his father's possessions. He couldn't manage his life better than his father. This is a good picture of the fact that a life lived outside God's will is a wasted life. This son ended up working for a Gentile and feeding pigs. This is also a good picture of how we end up serving other things when we refuse to be obedient to God. What is the good news in the text? What is the good news for our time?

We can never be independent. We will always serve something, either God or money as Jesus said in the Sermon on the Mount. This son had to go to the pigpen. This is how dirty he had to get, how low he had to sink. He was out of fellowship with his father; he had no one to enforce the rules or guide his walk and talk. Ultimately, he came to his senses and realized that he was wrong. He would go home and see if his father would at least let him work as a servant. At home, he saw the world as a great place, and there was so much fun he could have. He did not let pride get in his way, nor did he hold onto his grudges hanging around in the back of his head. He thought very smartly and decided to go home. There were rules there, but no pigs. He said to himself, *In my father's house, the servants are better off.* He began to recognize his situation. Can we recognize our situation? The past: Embrace it.

In an old episode of Andy Griffith, a man Andy sent to prison was getting out of jail. He was coming to town, and he sent word to Andy that he wanted to see him. Well, at first, Andy didn't think anything about it, but Barney made a big deal out of it. He told Andy that the man was probably gunning for him for revenge. Barney engaged Goober and Gomer to be deputies, and even Aunt Bee and Opie started to get a little nervous.

The man came to town carrying a long bag that looked like a shotgun. He came to Andy's house, and as he was coming up the walk,

Barney, Gomer, and Goober were panicking. Andy himself had gotten nervous by then. But the man reached into his bag and pulls out a gift for Andy. He had come to thank Andy because if Andy had not arrested him, his life would have never changed.

In the culture from which our text originates, stories have been told that if a son was bad and left home and then returned home, the father would have been expected to stone him, turn him away, or make him a slave. It was such a grave offense because to ask for his inheritance and to leave with it meant in essence that his father was dead to him. Having done that would have brought great disgrace upon his father. This was a bad Jewish boy, and an example needed to be made of him. If that was the case, the son was hoping for the last option—becoming his father's slave, as he mentioned in verses 17–19 of the text.

There has not been much change since then. If one of our children left home like that, would we disown them? We might talk down to such a child and never say anything encouraging so he or she would come back home. We would look at what he or she had and gave up to live on the streets, but it's much deeper than that.

The father diligently watched for and anticipated the return of this lost son. When he sees his son coming, he runs to meet him. In this culture, it was undignified for a man to run, but this father was not concerned with losing face. Jesus came to earth to find us and was willing to lose face. He suffered the most humiliating death known to man.[15]

The beauty of this text is the father, who let his son go knowing that he would fail and hoping that he would come back. This shows the graciousness and patience of the father. It is never too late to go back. Jesus is standing there with outstretched arms ready to welcome us back just like the father in our text.

---

[15] https://bible.org/seriespage/12-lost-sheep-coin-and-sons.

When the son returned, he rejoiced. Notice in verse 22 that the father interrupted the son before the son could pledge his service. All that is required is repentance and return, not works. The younger son may not have had full repentance when he was in the pig farm. He wanted to come back and work for his father maybe with the hope that he might be able to earn enough money to buy back his part of the land. But when he saw his father's humiliating sprint down the road toward him, saw what he had done to his father, saw his father's unconditional acceptance, and saw the lavish gifts his father bestowed on him, he recognized his father's goodness and realized that he could never earn his father's favor or inheritance; it was already his. He just needed to accept it. Those of us who are in trouble can approach the Father. The past ... Embrace it.

This parable of the lost son shows what kind of repentance the Father responds to and the way he responds to repentance by embracing the past. He didn't think about why his son had left, how much he had hurt him, or what had happened after he left; he was just so glad that his lost son was now found.

The son returning shows the healing of their relationship. Renewed relationships are what we need. We have a forgiving, loving God who does not keep score. He casts all of the old things that we need to have forgiven into the sea of forgetfulness.

By letting go of the past and embracing the future, we should be willing to forgive others. To whom much is given, much is required. It is the same way with grace.

Well, our young musician headed home. Before he could get down the end of his street, his father saw him coming and ran out to meet him. He hugged and kissed him with joy. While he tried to apologize to his father, his father called for someone to bring his son some new clothes and shoes, and he even gave him the ring his father had given him when he went off to college. He put steaks on the grill, ordered cakes, and got some of the best wine. The best musicians around came over and played. The father invited everyone in the neighborhood over for a big welcome home party; he said, "I thought my son was dead, and he is alive. He was lost, but now I've found him." They had one big party.

Let's celebrate by embracing those who have wronged us and releasing ourselves and them of the need to continue in pain and suffering. We must come to the Father and confess our sins. He is faithful and just to forgive us our sins and to cleanse us from all unrighteousness. All we have to do is come just like the lost son did. If we confess with our mouths, he will bring us back into the place of fellowship with him.

(I acknowledge bible.org from the series: The Parables, 12 The Lost Sheep, Coins and Sons for some of the imagery and language, especially in the beginning few paragraph of this sermon.)

The Past: Kiss It Goodbye
Text: Genesis 37:23–28, 45:12–15
Key Verse: Genesis 45:15

> And he kissed all his brothers and wept over them. Afterward his brothers talked with him. (Genesis 45:15 NIV)

> So when Joseph came to his brothers, they stripped him of his robe—the richly ornamented robe he was wearing—and they took him and threw him into the cistern. The cistern was empty; there was no water in it. As they sat down to eat their meal, they looked up and saw a caravan of Ishmaelites coming from Gilead. Their camels were loaded with spices, balm and myrrh, and

they were on their way to take them down to Egypt. Judah said to his brothers, "What will we gain if we kill our brother and cover up his blood? Come, let's sell him to the Ishmaelites and not lay our hands on him; after all, he is our brother, our own flesh and blood." His brothers agreed. So when the Midianite merchants came by, his brothers pulled Joseph up out of the cistern and sold him for twenty shekels of silver to the Ishmaelites, who took him to Egypt. (Genesis 37:23–28 NIV)

"You can see for yourselves, and so can my brother Benjamin, that it is really I who am speaking to you. Tell my father about all the honor accorded me in Egypt and about everything you have seen. And bring my father down here quickly." Then he threw his arms around his brother Benjamin and wept, and Benjamin embraced him, weeping. And he kissed all his brothers and wept over them. Afterward his brothers talked with him. (Genesis 45:12–15 NIV)

This is the third sermon in a series of on forgiveness and how the past can keep us from being fruitful now and block our future if we let it. We've heard, The Past: Face It, and The Past: Embrace It, and our theme today is The Past: Kiss It Goodbye. This is what Joseph did. Let us explore how he arrived there.

Have you ever heard the saying, "Just kiss and make up"? It may sound silly, but if you think about it, there is something to be said for it. When you've had a dispute with someone, a handshake, a hug, or a kiss seems to bring back into the relationship what had been lost. After parents discipline their children, the children might go away and sulk, but the minute their parents give them a hug or a kiss, their spirits seem to lift and they experience the forgiveness that their parents had just given them. The hugs seem to ease the hurt that the children had experienced, the hurt that came as a result of disappointing their parents by their behavior. (A touch restores the closeness of the relationship.) The same thing happens when a couple has an argument. The touch can bring about reconciliation. With coworkers and business partners, a handshake will go a long way in putting the past behind you. It is a way of answering the unspoken question, "Are we okay?" by affirming through the human connection of touch that we are indeed okay.

In our text, Joseph kisses his brothers, but let's look back at the story. The size of the family doesn't matter. Jealousy has a way of raising its ugly head. There are times when it makes you so sick that the only way to get relief is to get rid of the source of discomfort. You don't have to physically kill someone to get him or her out of your hair; you can simply just leave them somewhere in harm's way and wish that nature would take its course. So it is with our characters in today's text.

Joseph was a victim of the worst kind of betrayal, the type perpetrated by those closest to you—your family or friends. In this case, it was his brothers. Because of their envy and jealousy, they wanted to get rid of him. Most of the brothers wanted to kill him, so they threw him in a pit and left him to die, but two of them convinced the others to sell him into slavery. Imagine yourself as Joseph afraid in a dark pit and hearing you brothers arguing over whether to leave you to die or sell you to a stranger as a slave. Joseph had a lot to be hurt, disappointed, and angry about.

In a matter of hours, he went from being his father's favorite son to being a slave in a foreign land, a place where people served different gods and where Hebrews weren't treated with dignity or respect. They were slaves. Joseph didn't just lose his coat of many colors; he didn't just lose his room at home and all his favorite things; he lost his family, his freedom, and his trust of those closest to him. When Joseph was pushed into the pit, sold into slavery, and his father was led to believe that he was dead, his whole life direction changed.

But God had a plan. He always has a plan. God doesn't leave our lives to chance or luck. He is involved in everything that happens to us. Those brothers never expected to have to face up to what they had done some day, and even if they did, they had been in fear about it for more than twenty years.

Now look at Joseph. He has risen to the number two position in the kingdom—second only to the king. Joseph was running things, and guess who came looking for help? As for his brothers, you've heard the old saying, "Be kind to the people you meet on the way up because they are the same people you'll see on the way down." God has a way of bringing you back to the place where you messed up and giving you a chance to get it right.

The brothers were hungry and scared because a famine was coming, and Joseph, the one they hated, the one they had wanted to hurt, the one they had wanted to kill, was the one who could help them. Have you ever been there? Have you ever hurt someone and ended up needing him or her for something? Have you ever been ugly to someone who ended up coming to your side when you were in need? Have you ever pushed someone away only to find out when everyone else walked away from you, he or she stood by you and held your hand? The one you ridiculed, the one you gossiped about, the one you ganged up on because everyone else was doing it and you went along, but then you're in trouble and need someone. The only one who can or will help is the one you've persecuted. My, my, my, but the story turns right here.

Joseph recognized them, but they didn't recognize him. Imagine what must have gone through his mind. What would you be thinking?

Some of us would be thinking, *Oh no. I know they didn't come looking for me to help them. Oh, so now they need me? Oh, you didn't want me around back then. What? You want me to help you? I don't think so.* Some of us would just really enjoy this, and Joseph must have had all those emotions running through his mind. He was probably in a position that he could really punish them for what they had done to him, but he didn't.

His joy at seeing his brothers and the hope of seeing his father again caused him to respond in a way that they would never have expected. (Sometimes the greater good.) His anger would not have been productive. A need for revenge would not have been productive either to Joseph, his father, or to his brothers. What happened to Joseph happened for a reason. It wasn't so that Joseph could suffer but so that he would be the instrument by which God would deliver his people. "God, make me an instrument of thy peace."

There was no need for Joseph to keep dragging around the pain and the hurt of the past. Since he had been in Egypt, God had been using him to prepare for a famine that would come and threaten the whole nation of Israel, so Joseph kissed the heartache of the past, the fear of the past, and the demons of the past goodbye.

Joseph exemplified God's forgiveness. We too must learn not to harbor a grudge. Because God has forgiven us, we can forgive others. He has a forgiving heart. What does it mean to have a heart like his? It means to kneel as Jesus knelt, touching the grimy parts of the people we are stuck with, and washing their unkindness with kindness.

When Joseph embraced and kissed his brothers after more than twenty years of separation, that began a process of release for Joseph and his brothers. When Joseph kissed his brothers, all the guilt and shame they had carried around started to fade. The touch of the one they harmed began to restore them. They wanted to flee from his sight, but the touch, the embrace, the kiss, held them there. It allowed them to start the healing process because wrapped up in that hug and kiss was all the baggage of the past ready to be cast into the sea of forgetfulness, the sea of forgiveness.

I'm so glad that it didn't stop with Joseph. Jesus, betrayed, hurt, disappointed, persecuted, and killed, didn't let us flee from his sight. He embraced us and said, "Father, forgive them, for they do not know what they are doing" (Luke 23:34a NIV).

What are we really saying? "I've done nothing wrong. I'm not the one who cheated. I'm not the one who is jealous. I'm not the one who lied. I'm not the guilty party here." Perhaps you aren't, but neither is Jesus. The genius of Jesus's example is that the burden of bridge building falls on the strong one, not the weak one. The one who is innocent is the one who makes the gesture, and you know what happens then. More often than not, if the one in the right volunteers to wash the feet of the one in the wrong, both parties get on their knees. Don't we all think we are right? Hence, we wash each other's feet. Relationships don't thrive because the guilty are punished; they thrive because the innocent are merciful. Joseph kissed his brothers and the past experiences goodbye.

Will you obey God and forgive? Pack up your pain, anger, and hurt and kiss them goodbye. You've carried it far too long. It's helped to shape who you are, but now it's time to move forward. Kiss it goodbye. You love company, but there comes a time when you kiss them goodbye. Your pain has been a familiar thing for you for some time, but the time is now to kiss it goodbye. God has something waiting on you, but you can't see around the pain of the past. Kiss it goodbye.

The past is blocking your vision. Kiss it goodbye. You can remember more of the past than you can of what's going on around you right now. Kiss it goodbye. Pack it up. Say, "It's been real, but you got to go!" The past … Kiss it goodbye.

APPENDIX B

Reconciliation: The Power of Working Together with Sincere Hearts
Text: Acts 2:42–47
Key Verse: Acts 2:46

> Every day they continued to meet together in the temple courts. They broke bread in their homes and ate together with glad and sincere hearts. (Acts 2:46 NIV)

> They devoted themselves to the apostles' teaching and to fellowship, to the breaking of bread and to prayer. Everyone was filled with awe at the many wonders and signs performed by the apostles. All the believers were together and had everything in common. They sold property and possessions to give to anyone who had need. Every day they continued to meet together in the temple courts. They broke bread in their homes and ate together with glad and sincere hearts, praising God and enjoying the favor of all the people. And the Lord added to their number daily those who were being saved. (Acts 2:42–27 NIV)

As we join this scene, Peter has just preached a sermon on repentance. He had called the people to responsibility and accountability for their part in the crucifixion of Jesus. He told the crowd that Jesus had been sent by God to perform miracles, wonders, and signs through the power of God, yet the people had not believed. Jesus had been persecuted and killed, and they had gone along with it.

When Peter had finished making his appeal to the people, the Bible says, "They were cut to the heart." They asked Peter, "What shall we do?" Peter said, "Repent, be baptized, and receive the Holy Spirit." He reminded them that the church was for all who were to come in the future—as many as the Lord would call.

We come to the point where the people have repented. They have begun to live faithfully in the apostles' doctrine. They have begun to engage in fellowship with each other—eating and praying together. Before this, they had not been of one accord. Some had believed in Jesus while others had not, and others were not concerned one way or the other. There had to be some pain, hurt, and even bitterness. When Peter preached to them, he convicted them all. Then they were of one accord—all those who repented and believed the Word of the Lord. The Holy Spirit could work in their lives.

What a grand future the church would have if we could learn to work together. The church is not just for us today but for our children's children and their children. It is for generations to come until Jesus returns. We must learn to work together to expand the kingdom of God. If we could just learn to not put aside but work through our differences, what a bold and bright light the church would be to the world. Well, how do we come to a place of working together in the power of the Holy Spirit? It is with sincere hearts, hearts of repentance and sorrow for poor decisions, disagreements, and lack of faith in God.

Too often, we get so stuck on the past that we shut down. We don't see past our pain and hurt. We give up all hope, but with sincere hearts, we can find our way to repentance and from repentance to reconciliation. When we have reconciled our differences, we can work together. Things may not be restored to their original state, but we can work together in the power of the Holy Spirit. After all, what had been done to Jesus had been done; he had suffered, died, and rose just as the scriptures had foretold. Giving up on expanding the kingdom would not have been the way God would have them live; that is not how God wants us to live.

I shared a portion of our text for this message with a young woman. I asked her, "What does it take to serve with a sincere heart?"

"Spiritual fitness," she said. "Discipline. Faith exercised regularly grows strong and electrifying. Faith ignored becomes weak and flabby like our bodies sometimes."

She shared that when she had her first child, she worked so hard to get that perfect shape. She did sit-ups and ran every day until she had a Coke-bottle shape. It was rough. Some mornings, she just didn't feel like doing sit-ups or running, but she would turn on the television and exercise anyway because it was good for her. It takes discipline to do this every day, and discipline is never easy, but the reward of feeling and looking good is worth it.

God wants us all to enroll in a spiritual fitness program. In our text, they devoted themselves to the apostles' teaching, and so must we. The apostles preached and taught the gospel, which of course focuses on Jesus Christ. Imagine them sitting at the apostles' feet hungry to receive instruction.

Is there anyone thirsty? To quench your thirst, you must acknowledge that it will not be and was not a ten-week or two-year course they participated in; it was something lifelong. It wasn't only the elderly but the middle aged and the youth too who had received instruction. They heard the Word, they studied it, memorized it, meditated on it, and spread it. Above all they, wholehearted lived it.

God wants us to enroll in a spiritual fitness program that included fellowship, which involves loving, caring, praying, and sharing. In this sin-filled world, it takes much sweat and dedication to experience genuine fellowship. Today, we often reduce fellowship to close friends or being friendly with one another. Genuine fellowship as revealed in our text is never easy or automatic; it requires sacrifice. Further, the Bible instructs us to be loving to one another, to encourage one another, to be devoted to one another, to build up one another, to be kind to one another, to serve one another, and to not judge one another. This gives way to the power that lies in working together.

The apostles were persistent, constant, and continuous in their prayer. Christians who want to be spiritually fit need to spend time in prayer because in prayer, we come to draw on God, his power, and his resources and make them ours for his glory. What a healthy church we have when we devote ourselves to teaching, fellowship, worship, and prayer. The scripture reveals to us that they were enjoying the favor of all the people, and the Lord added to their number daily those who were being saved. Are we ready for an increase?

It's all in the power of working together. Since they have learned to work together and to live together taking care of each other and those along the way, all the needs of the people are being met. Not only that; because of their visible witness, people are watching and wanting to be a part of this wonderful thing. What if we could learn to live together, to work together, to pray together, and to serve together? What power that would be.

If we focused on the task that God has set before us rather than our differences, we could see more and more people wanting to be a part of the body of Christ. What's holding us back from working together with others, from being team players? What do we need to repent of so we can again experience the joy of ministry? What grieves us so that we can't sing the praises of God like we used to do? What holds us back from fellowship with our brothers and sisters in Christ? What are you saying that could cause others to turn from the body? Are you drawing others or repelling them? What if you had a sincere heart? The benefits of working together with sincere hearts will show up; the Holy Spirit will have room to lead, guide, direct, and draw us.

What can we learn from the Christians in the early church? They were living uncomplicated lives, praising God, and having favor with all the people. Likewise, we are called to see all the people. Their hearts were in their service, their walks were sincere, their fellowship was real, and their living was above reproach. Solomon wrote in Ecclesiastes 4:9–10 (NKJV), "Two are better than one, because they have a good reward for their labor. For if they fall, one will lift up his companion. But woe to him who is alone when he falls; for he has no one to help him up." The power of working together overcomes the selfish individual who works in competition with others. Yes, even in the church. They miss the reward of being in fellowship with one another the way God created humans to be—in companionship and community with God and each another.

With sincere hearts, we can throw a party for that lost son who has made his way back home. With sincere hearts, we can sit with those who have caused us so much pain and disappointment because they committed themselves into drug rehab. With sincere hearts, we can work with those who would betray us and seek to destroy us because we will be looking for the good in them, praying for them, and allowing the Holy Spirit to work in God's timing.

With a sincere heart, you can extend a helping hand to those in need without judging them for their circumstances. With sincere hearts, we will make time to visit those who are sick and shut-in, feed the hungry, clothe those who need that, and stand up against injustice and oppression in whatever form they take.

Now is the time when true worshipers will worship the Father in spirit and truth, for they are the kind of worshipers the Father seeks (John 4:23). The early church worshipers embodied such worship in spirit and truth with sincere hearts.

The Power of Working Together
It's a Ministry
Text: 2 Corinthians 5:16–21
Key Verse: 2 Corinthians 5:17–18

> Therefore, if anyone is in Christ, he is a new creation: The old has gone, the new has come! All this is from God, who reconciled us to himself through Christ and gave us the ministry of reconciliation. (2 Corinthians 5:17–18 NIV)

> So from now on we regard no one from a worldly point of view. Though we once regarded Christ in this way, we do so no longer. Therefore, if anyone is in Christ, he is a new creation: The old has gone, the new has come! All this is from God, who reconciled us to himself through Christ and gave us the ministry of reconciliation: that God was reconciling the world to himself in Christ, not counting people's sins against them. And he has committed to us the message of reconciliation. We are therefore Christ's ambassadors, as though God were making his appeal through us. We implore you on Christ's behalf: Be reconciled to God. God made him who had no sin to be sin[b] for us, so that in him we might become the righteousness of God. (2 Corinthians 5:16–21 NIV)

If we say we forgive others but are never able to look at or interact with them without thinking of or bringing up what has happened in the past, have we truly forgiven them? If we say that what is in the past is in the past, do we really mean it?

Let me share a story with you. There was a woman in a priest's parish who deeply loved God and claimed to have visions in which she spoke with Christ and he spoke with her. As might be expected, the priest was skeptical of her claims, so to test her visions, he said to her, "You say you actually speak with Christ in your visions. Let me ask you a favor. The next time you have one of these visions, I want you to ask him what sin I committed while in seminary."

The woman agreed to that. When she returned to the church a few days later, the priest asked, "Well, did Christ visit you in your dream?"

"Yes he did," she replied.

"And did you ask what sin I committed in seminary?"

"Yes, I asked him," she answered. "He told me, 'I don't remember.'"

I share this story with you because we are called to a ministry of reconciliation. Let us use for a subject The Power of Working Together: It's a Ministry.

To reconcile means that we work to restore harmony and settle or resolve disputes and disagreements. In our text, Paul revealed to us that God had given us a ministry, one of reconciliation. Our calling is to help restore the breaches that exist and be ambassadors for Jesus Christ. Ambassadors are representatives of the one who sends them on assignment. If we are ambassadors for Christ, we are his representatives, and we are to present his case and cause and model him as well. Christ, who demonstrated love and forgiveness for those who persecuted and humiliated him, forgave and extended grace even to those who caused him fatal harm.

In our text, Paul lifted up to us the fact that we have been recipients of God's reconciliation and should therefore model and minister to others that same spirit of grace and reconciliation. Because of God's love for us, Christ came to reconcile humanity to God. Christ demonstrates that forgiveness for us. The problem comes when we ambassadors are unable to extend to others the grace and mercy that God has extended to us. We often run away from what has taken place and live in a false reality that produces shallow relationships that bear no fruit. We bear no fruit because when we have broken fellowship that remains unattended to, we cannot experience the power of working together. It's a ministry, and ministry calls for sacrifice and making ourselves vulnerable in order to move forward.

As long as we continue to hold others' faults, failures, and sins against them, we are not moving toward reestablishing relationships in which we can move forward. As long as we continue to hold other's faults, failures, and sins against them, we are not modeling the ministry of Jesus and being his ambassadors. We are not following the example that Jesus made for us. Oh there is power in working together. It's a ministry!

Jesus showed us the love God has for us and for all creation, which is at the heart of the redemption work that Jesus came to do. Even when we don't think that any difference can be made, we can look to God and see how he will take what is broken and mold it, shape it, and make it into something that can be used to bring about healing.

I am reminded of a story about a young man named Paco who found himself separated from his family. No one could really say whether he had run away or if he had been kicked out of his home by his father for something he had done. The point is that Paco was out on the streets of Madrid chasing after his dream of bullfighting. Some who train hard and have others working to help them can be successful in this profession, but for others, it can be suicide.

Out of concern for his son, Paco's father began to search for him, but Madrid was so large. After giving it some thought, his father decided to run an advertisement in the newspaper that read, "Paco, meet me at the Hotel Montana at noon on Tuesday. All is forgiven! Love, Papa."[16]

Paco is a most common name in Spain. When the father went to the hotel to meet his son, there were eight hundred young men named Paco waiting for their fathers and to reconcile with them, something they had thought would never take place.

Like God in our text, Paco's father took the initiative in reconciling the broken relationship with his son. When we, like Paco, were out wandering and wondering which way to turn, God sought us out and drew us in so that we might be brought back into relationship with him. No matter what had happened, Paco had a desire to be in right relationship with his father, and so did nearly eight hundred other Pacos. That doesn't take into consideration the young men whose names were Pablo, José, or Jesús. Our need to make ourselves vulnerable, humble ourselves, and go back to the place where we got off track is not something that is limited to just a few individuals; it is necessary for many of us. When we realize the power of working together, we understand that it is a ministry.

We realize that it requires us to humble ourselves. Then, we don't seek to be right but to be righteous, and that can be found only in Jesus Christ. Who among us has a broken relationship? I wonder if anyone here has a Paco, a Maria, a mother, father, sister, brother, spouse, friend, or someone else from whom they are separated and their pride won't let them reach out to them. Well, Paco's father realized that life was precious and too short to take for granted. More than that, he realized

---

[16] https://philipchircop.wordpress.com/2012/07/05/paco-all-is-forgiven/.

that he valued the relationship with his son more than anything else, so he reached out.

My sisters and brothers, God values you over and above anything else. The Bible tells us that he created us just a little lower than the angels and considers us highly. The Bible also tells us that God loved us so much that he sent his only Son, Jesus, so that whoever believed in him would not perish but have everlasting life. Jesus makes our relationship right with God. When we can accept him as our Lord and Savior, we can realize the common ground on which we stand.

Working together is a ministry because we can be out here alone and lost, not knowing where to turn, or we can realize that we are in this thing called life together and let go of the things that are separating us and move forward together.

So what will you do? Will you think about the relationships that you need to work on to improve? Will you reach out to those who have hurt you so that you can move forward?

Reconciliation is a ministry, and it's in your heart. I believe when they returned home, the family was waiting, longtime friends were waiting, the elders of the community were there, the table was prepared, and a celebration was on for all who were waiting for the good news. And it was indeed good news. The ministry of reconciliation began on Calvary when Jesus said, "Father forgive them for they know not what they do." He went down to the grave … and early, one morning … he rose up with all power in his hand … It's a ministry of victory. It's a ministry of reconciliation. It's a ministry of transformation. It's a ministry that calls all together for the common good of all humanity. Can I get an amen?

The Power of Working Together
Text: Nehemiah 1:3–6, 4:6
Key Verse: Nehemiah 4:6

> So we rebuilt the wall till all of it reached half its height, for the people worked with all their heart. (Nehemiah 4:6 NIV)

> They said to me, "Those who survived the exile and are back in the province are in great trouble and disgrace. The wall of Jerusalem is broken down, and its gates have been burned with fire." When I heard these things, I sat down and wept. For some days I mourned and fasted and prayed before the God of heaven. Then I said: "Lord, the God of heaven, the great and awesome God, who keeps his covenant of love with those who love him and keep his commandments, let your ear be attentive and your eyes open to hear the prayer your servant is praying before you day and night for your servants, the people of Israel. I confess the sins we Israelites, including myself and my father's family, have committed against you." (Nehemiah 1:3–6 NIV)

Have you ever felt comfortable and safe in your home but just outside, right there in your community, you know that there was work to be done for the ministry of God? Nehemiah was in such a position. He was wearing the robe of royalty. He was the king's cupbearer. He was in a position of power, but his heart beat for the people in Israel. He was a Hebrew in Persia.

When word reached him concerning the condition of Jerusalem and the people, Nehemiah invited God to use him; he prayed,

I confess the sins we Israelites, including myself and my father's house, have committed against you. We acted very wickedly toward you. We have not obeyed the commands, decrees and laws you gave your servants Moses.

After his prayer, Nehemiah exchanged the royal robe for coveralls and got to work.

The Power of Working Together

In our text, the scripture tells us that Nehemiah went back to Jerusalem. His heart had been moved to rebuild the city, and he had a vision of what could be done. He started to get different groups of people to rebuild the defensive walls of Jerusalem. Their height and thickness depended on the potential threat to the city and the resources it had. The wall of Jericho was a famous biblical wall. The Bible tells us that it could not be penetrated or trespassed by any human force, but we know how that story went when God allowed a few of the men in the army of the Lord to just march around the city and shout; the walls collapsed.

The walls of the city are intended for its protection, but there is a flipside to that. While walls are intended to keep some out, they are also used to keep others in. What that means spiritually is that a wall could have represented two things.

First, the lack of attention that had been given to the city had caused its protection to be lost. The city was at that point vulnerable and open. What that means for us in this journey of reconciliation is that while we have allowed the breaches to grow wider and wider between us, we have allowed ourselves and others to be left open to the attacks of the enemy. God will keep a hedge around us, but when we walk in broken fellowship with each other and thus broken fellowship with God, we are outside his hedge of protection. Nehemiah, therefore, confessed the sins of the people before God day and night with the hope that God would forgive and reconcile them to himself and to each other.

Second, walls or barriers prevent people having fellowship or relationship with each other. Many of us when we encounter problems in a relationship will put up a barrier of some kind so that we can protect ourselves from being hurt again. We may become unapproachable, hardened, or cold in some ways, and we may refuse to participate in certain things in which we once found great joy. All of this is because we have failed to forgive and to reconcile ourselves to our brother or sister so that we could continue walking together and working toward pointing others to God's kingdom.

The wall was in ruins because of the refusal to keep it up by being obedient to God's Word and living in harmony with one another and even God. It was in ruins because we have refused to cast down those walls that keep us divided and in broken fellowship with one another and even with God. When we realize the power of working together, we know that walls of unforgiveness cause us to focus on the pain rather than on the ministry to which God has called us.

God had their attention. They could no longer hide behind the walls, and they could no longer keep others out. They were at the point where they had no choice thanks be to God but to work together.

Chapter 3 tells us how the city wall was rebuilt. Just imagine this: an earthquake came through Kershaw County. It took out I-20 from exit 103 to the county line. We are just devastated because some of us can't go to work or our drive will be very hectic. The governor, our Nehemiah, flew over the interstate in his helicopter with the lieutenant governor as his pilot. After observing the damages, he gave a televised speech to the citizens of Kershaw County. He was very touched and felt deep down in his heart that we could recover from this. While he was speaking, tears were rolling down from his eyes. He said, "Everyone must pull together and come out tomorrow so that we can rebuild our interstate."

The next day, the governor was the first one on I-20 working with his staff from the county line toward exit 82. Then African-Americans started to rebuild the next section, exit 82 toward exit 87. Then the Hispanic community started to work on the next section. A group of white people started to work on the rest area and the next section.

Keep on looking down I-20 because there are people who hadn't spoken to each other in years working together rebuilding the bridges, there are those who were in captivity in their inner thoughts working together rebuilding the Camden exit ramp. There are the rich and poor working together all the way down the exit. There are people from every walk of life, of every color, of every socioeconomic status, of every religious or faith affiliation all working together.

And so it is the people rebuilt a small section of the wall of Jerusalem. After two days, the whole wall around the city had been built by persons or groups rebuilding the wall bit by bit. And that is the way it is done. If you want to rebuild the life of a nation, a city, a family, or yourself, you cannot do it alone. You need help. And people need to help a little bit. If you are rebuilding your life or your family, you need to draw in the help of a grandparent, a parent, a pastor, a Sunday school teacher, a friend, and a neighbor. If you are trying to put your life together after a disaster, you need all kinds of people to help you a little bit.

The power of working together and the prayer of Nehemiah helped the people to remember that their strength was in the joy of the Lord. We all have difficult assignments accompanied by feelings of inadequacy; however, all things can be accomplished by staying connected to God through prayer—every day and in every situation through dependence on God and devotion to his Word. Nehemiah reminded the exiles of their spiritual heritage and encouraged them to successfully rebuild the city wall. There is true power in working together for the good of the Lord's kingdom.

Come to God. Tell God that you want to be a Nehemiah, that you want a close relationship with him. You no longer want to be in captivity in your inner thoughts, to the past, or to what others may want to say or how they may say it. You want to be in prayer for yourself and others. You want to do your part, your little bit. That's the power of working together—you, you, and you doing it from your heart. Doing your little bit freely.

Transformation: Being Transformed
Text: Romans 12:1–2
Key Verse: 12:2

> Therefore, I urge you, brothers, in view of God's mercy, to offer your bodies as a living sacrifice, holy and pleasing to God—this is your spiritual act of worship. Do not conform any longer to the pattern of this world, but be transformed by the renewing of your mind. Then you will be able to test and approve what God's will is —his good, pleasing and perfect will. (Romans 12:1–2 NIV)

Over the past two years, I have preached several sermons to you on forgiveness and reconciliation. These sermons have called us to face our hurts and move on from them into the future to which God is calling us. However, we are not there just yet because we still remember, we still hold onto, too much of the past.

The world tells us, "I'll forgive you, but I won't forget." God says to us that he casts our sins into the sea of forgetfulness never to be remembered. If we want to truly move on and be made whole, we have to change our way of thinking. We have to allow ourselves to be transformed. We do that by renewing our minds. We replace our way of seeing and doing things with the way God calls us to see and do things. If we want to be on our way to restoration, if we want to be living sacrifices, if we want to cast off the weights that are holding us down, we must allow transformation to take place. Transformation is what the scripture calls for this morning.

Let's explore the word *transformation*, for which the Greek word is *fashioning*. Webster's defines transformation as an act, a process of changing. It's like the television shows *The Transformers*, *Power Rangers*, *Superman*, or *Spiderman*. They changed into various superheroes, but let us not get confused here because that was a change on the outside that took place. When they first found out they had these super powers, a change was made on the inside. They wanted to save or help others, so they put their lives in danger to do that. It was never about them in any situation but always about saving the world or an individual. They had a change on the inside first before they took on these changes on the outside.

Let's break this down.

1. Transformation is defined as an act. Now, act is an action word meaning something you can see—you know the difference in a person; the color of their hair, clothes, the way they treated you yesterday versus today. We saw that in these superheroes; there was a change in their clothes, their outer appearance.

2. To be transformed is also an action word, but it's on the inside, not the outside. When someone found out about these superheroes' powers, they would try to sell them to get money or make them very powerful. But these superheroes would always end up rescuing the person who sold them out. Yes, they would

get mad and find out why they did it, but then they would save them. Do they carry this until the next time? No. They repeatedly saved people like this.

That is what our God almighty does—he saves us repeatedly because he loves us and wants us to be living and holy sacrifices; he does not want us to copy the behavior and customs of this world. Instead, he desires a change that takes place on the inside that the outside reflects. We should not be holding grudges against someone or still be angry because of something that happened five, ten, or fifteen years ago. We need to know how to approach and talk with our sisters and brothers; we need to love spiritually and mentally in spite of; we can't do these things on our own. We need to sit at the feet of Jesus.

When we are living with unforgiveness, it affects us in a number of ways. It affects our emotional states, our physical health, and our social lives. Most important, it affects our spiritual lives. Walking in unforgiveness affects our worship and can cause us to put up a wall between us and God. We cannot worship God in spirit and truth when we have division between us and our brother or sister. We must be transformed because we are called to be transformed. Transformation is our way to restoration. But how can forgiveness transform us?

When we let go of hurt, bitterness, and emotional baggage, we allow joy to once again become a part of our lives. We find ourselves viewing life with a renewed outlook, and we can laugh. We no longer feel the need to carry around the heaviness of depression that we once allowed to become a major part of our lives. We begin to find ourselves again, and restoration can then begin to take place. This is the transformation that takes place when we forgive each other, reconcile our differences, and allow the Word of God and the grace of our Lord and Savior Jesus

Christ to replace the old way of thinking, the old way of doing, the old conforming to this world.

We allow our minds and hearts to be changed by renewing our minds or replacing the old resentment and bitterness from the past with the new mercies that God gives to us daily. "A renewed mind is essential to the discernment of God's will and the transformation of life."[17]

In our text, Paul spoke of the mercies of God. If God is able to be merciful toward us no matter what we have done, shouldn't we be able to be merciful to one another?

In the news over the past weeks, we have heard about the Jenna Six, young men who were facing long jail sentences for what amounted to a fight that came as a result of racism in a small town. It all began under a tree that was supposed to be for white students only. Well, some black students decided that they wanted to gather under the tree. When they did so, several nooses were hung on the tree. This led to a fight between some of the white boys and some of the black boys, and things escalated. Now, it has gained national attention as one of the young men was facing twenty years or so in prison. The outcome has been that the charges have been reduced. And the town is cutting down the tree.

What will cutting down the tree do to bring about healing in this town and all over the nation as many have felt offended by this mishandling of the justice system? Cutting down the tree is a way of eliminating the visible sign of the problem, but unless hearts are changed, it won't bring about forgiveness and reconciliation. It will only take out of sight the same problem that has remained hidden in this small town for many, many years.

Wouldn't it be a good thing if the tree rather than being cut down could have become a place of fellowship for those who could learn to move past their hurt, anger, and disappointment and learn to live

---

[17] *The New Interpreter's Study Bible*, 2028.

together in peace and harmony. Wouldn't it be a good thing if rather than cutting down the tree, we renewed our minds through the Word of God that calls us to love our neighbors as ourselves and cut away the hate and prejudice that cause us to be divided. Wouldn't it be good if rather than cutting down the tree, we cut down the influence of those who would continue to use political gain and media exposure to exploit the errors in judgment in young people who are looking to adults for leadership and teaching. Wouldn't it be good if rather than cutting down the tree, we cut away the ugliness that we allow to creep into our hearts when we are divided against each other.

We could go around harboring and carrying resentment from slavery and racism that took place many, many years ago (and some do), or we could learn to work through our differences as much as we can and allow the rest to go so that we can be healed in our hearts, minds, and souls.

When we renew our minds, we begin to think differently; we begin to notice the sun shining a little brighter, the birds singing a little louder, and the flowers smelling a little stronger. We learn to breathe in deeply the sweetness of life that we had allowed to become stale and stagnant. And each time we allow ourselves to be catalysts for forgiveness and healing, we become stronger. We are no longer like the world, but we become Christ like. Doing what is easy is natural, but doing what is Christ like is supernatural. And when we allow ourselves to tap into that part of us that defies all of what would make us feel better and cost us less time, energy, dignity, and pride, we are being transformed never to be the same again.

When we allow God to transform us, we can begin to become what God would have us to be, "that which is acceptable." We can be made whole. We can be healthy physically, emotionally, and spiritually. We can have the joy we once knew back in our lives. This is what happens when we allow God to change our way of thinking, renew our minds, and transform us from the ways of this world into the way that he needs us to be for the world to come.[18]

Are you longing to be restored? Have you felt as if you are dragging around a heavy load that you would like to leave behind? The Bible tells us to cast our care on Jesus for he cares for us. Jesus is calling us today to be transformed, to allow him to renew our minds so we can be transformed into all that God would have us be. Don't you want your joy back? Don't you want your love back? Don't you want your bounce back in your step? Don't you want your shoulders to stand out straight? Don't you want to have that laughter back in your eyes and a smile on your lips? Then it is time to get yourself into the Word of God and your prayer closet. It is time to let yourself be freed of the burdens that have you cast down. It is time to live again. There is a wall hanging in a store that says, "It's never too late to live happily ever after."

An Encounter with God: An Encounter with Forgiveness
Text: Acts 9:1–9
Key Verse: Acts 9:5

> "Who are you, Lord?" Saul asked. "I am Jesus, whom you are persecuting," he replied. (Acts 9:5 NIV)

> Meanwhile, Saul was still breathing out murderous threats against the Lord's disciples. He went to the high priest and asked him for letters to the synagogues in Damascus, so that if he found any there who belonged to the Way, whether men or women, he might take them as prisoners to Jerusalem. As he neared Damascus on his journey, suddenly a light from heaven flashed

---

[18] *The Interpreter's Bible*, volume 9. Nashville: Abingdon Press, 1954.

around him. He fell to the ground and heard a voice say to him," Saul, Saul, why do you persecute me?" "Who are you, Lord?" Saul asked. "I am Jesus, whom you are persecuting," he replied." Now get up and go into the city, and you will be told what you must do." The men traveling with Saul stood there speechless; they heard the sound but did not see anyone. Saul got up from the ground, but when he opened his eyes he could see nothing. So they led him by the hand into Damascus. For three days he was blind, and did not eat or drink anything. (Acts 9:1–9 NIV)

An Encounter with God

An encounter, according to *Webster's*, is to come upon face to face or to come upon someone or something unexpectedly. In our text, Saul had aggressively persecuted the church of God.

He tracked down Christians as they fled from his attack. Saul was determined to keep the kingdom pure, and that simply meant keeping the Christians out. However, all of this came to a halt on the road to Damascus. That's when the light came on, that's when unconditional love met him, and Saul heard the voice. He prayed that death would be quick and painless., But all he got was silence and the first of a lifetime of surprise. He ended up bewildered and befuddled in a borrowed bedroom. God left him there a few days with scales on his eyes so thick that the only direction he could look was inside. And he didn't like what he saw. He saw himself for what he really was—to use his own words, the worst of sinners. Alone in the room with his sins on his conscience and blood on his hand, he asked to be cleansed.[19]

---

[19] Lucado, Max. *The Applause of Heaven*. Nashville, Tennessee, by Thomas Nelson1999, 40.

In order to fulfill his purpose, Saul needed to confess, repent, and come to an understanding of God's will for his life. We need to acknowledge our faults, release our hurts, seek forgiveness, and reconcile with ourselves, God, and humanity. Our text seems to suggest that this leads to transformation.

Saul's encounter with the Lord on the road to Damascus led to his complete transformation from the inside out. His name was changed after his eyes were opened. Paul was never the same afterward, and neither was the world around him. It was on that trip that God saved Saul. It took God's power to save a sinner like Saul, and it takes God's transforming power to save sinners like you and me. A close encounter with God always leaves an unforgettable impression. The result of it just may be so great that the whole world is transformed by the conversion of a sinner. The text reveals an encounter with God, an encounter with forgiveness.

It can be said that Paul never expected to need the help of Ananias. As a matter of fact, he never expected to need the help of any Christian. Sometimes, our help comes from the most unlikely places. Do you remember the former governor of Alabama, the late George Wallace? Well, let me tell you. George Wallace was an up-and-coming political superstar. He had it all going for him. People followed him because of his ability to energize and excite them. The problem was that he was defending a system that kept African-American students from going to school with white students.

He wanted and defended a system that kept black people and white people separated, and in Alabama, the law was very well enforced. Rosa Parks went to jail for sitting too close to the front of a bus. Wallace said that as long as he was standing, he would defend the segregation laws of Alabama, which were laws that separated blacks and whites in schools and in public areas such as restrooms, water fountains, and restaurants.

He became so popular that he ran for president, but Wallace wouldn't be standing very long because a gunman tried to take his life, and he ended up in a wheelchair.

Forced to sit in a wheelchair, George Wallace had plenty to think about. He ended up confessing his guilt over the deaths of John F. Kennedy, Robert Kennedy, and Martin Luther King. He ended up confessing that his heart had been in all the wrong places. This is a true story of forgiveness, reconciliation, and transformation because Wallace changed so much that he ran for governor again in Alabama and was reelected. Where do you think a large number of his votes came from? African-Americans. He went on to be a friend of African-Americans for the rest of his life. When forgiveness and reconciliation take place, hearts are changed and transformation happens. We can become new creations. An encounter with God is an encounter with forgiveness.

There is a story of a missionary in the United Methodist Church who because his bishop had served in Vietnam felt the need for his conference to be in ministry there. During a worship service, a man with only one arm said that he had been captured and tortured by the Vietnamese. When he tried to escape, a soldier shot his arm off at close range to teach him a lesson. The man sitting in the pew next to him said, "I am the soldier that shot him. He has forgiven me and God has forgiven me. Because of the mercy and grace given to me, I am changed."

An encounter with God is indeed an encounter with forgiveness; you are never the same after one of those encounters. In the name of the Father and of the Son and the Holy Spirit, the people of God said, amen.

REFERENCES

The New Open Bible, New King James Version. Thomas Nelson Publishers, 1993.

Barker, Kenneth, ed. The NIV Study Bible. Grand Rapids, MI: Zondervan, 1995.

The Concise American Heritage Dictionary, revised edition. Houghton Mifflin, 1987.

Merriam-Webster's Collegiate Dictionary, tenth edition, 2001.

Jones, Gregory L. *Embodying Forgiveness: A Theological Analysis*. Grand Rapids, MI: Eerdmans, 1995.

Edgerton, W. Dow. *O Speak to Me That I May Speak: A Spirituality of Preaching*. Cleveland: Pilgrim Press, 2006.

The Holy Bible, New Revised Standard Version. Nashville: World Publishing, 1989.

Thomas, Frank A. *They Like to Never Quit Praisin' God: The Role of Celebration in Preaching*. New York: Pilgrim Press, 1997.

The Open Bible, New King James Version. Thomas Nelson, 1982.

The Interpreter's Study Bible, volume 9. Nashville: Abingdon Press, 2003.

Jones, Kirk Byron. *The Jazz of Preaching: How to Preach with Freedom and Joy*. Nashville: Abingdon Press, 2004.

Lucado, Max. *The Applause of Heaven*. Nashville, Tennessee, by Thomason Nelson 1999

Lightning Source UK Ltd.
Milton Keynes UK
UKHW012049120821
388784UK00008B/466/J